AIR CRASH

Northumberland

Russell Gray
Jim Corbett
Jonathan Shipley
Neil Anderson

COUNTRYSIDE BOOKS
NEWBURY BERKSHIRE

First published 2008

COUNTRYSIDE BOOKS
3 Catherine Road
Newbury, Berkshire

To view our complete range of books,
please visit us at
www.countrysidebooks.co.uk

ISBN 978 1 84674 112 8

Designed by Peter Davies, Nautilus Design
Produced through MRM Associates Ltd., Reading
Printed by Cambridge University Press

All material for the manufacture of this book
was sourced from sustainable forests

CONTENTS

INTRODUCTION

As members of the Air Crash Investigation and Archaeology group (ACIA), our aim is to research and study the remains of aircraft crashes in northern England and southern Scotland, with the intention of preserving the memory of the people who lost their lives in these tragic accidents. With the help of local historians, eyewitness accounts and careful, detailed analysis of historical documents, we are able to piece together the last moments of an aircraft's flight and bring to public attention the existence of a crash site which in many instances has faded from memory. When published, such knowledge can often enable relatives of the aircrew involved to learn more of their fate and even the location of their final resting place.

The research we have undertaken has led us to work with local authorities, in particular the county archaeologists, to determine the best methods for recovering aircraft remains and correctly recording what we have found. The correct recording of aircraft remains is particularly important as it provides future researchers, as well as the general public, with an archive detailing the locations of numerous crash sites throughout the north-east, along with information relating to each loss.

In certain circumstances the target crash site may provide remains that are recoverable. Where this is possible and identifiable artefacts can be retrieved, permission is sought from the Ministry of Defence; if granted, parts are recovered and catalogued with the express purpose of putting them on public display rather than being held in private collections. To this end we always work with local museums, heritage centres, etc in order to bring our hobby to a wider audience.

Investigation of a particular crash site can have wide-ranging consequences and can touch the lives of many people, not just in Great Britain but across the world. Airmen who lost their lives during the Second World War came not just from Great Britain but from all over the Commonwealth and the United States, while others managed to escape from occupied countries in Europe to take up the fight. One need only visit the cemetery of St Mary and St James in Morpeth to see a host of graves for airmen from New Zealand, Poland, the Netherlands and Belgium, all buried far from their homeland. We must also remember the many German airmen who lost their lives in the skies over the north, or in the cold waters of the North Sea. These young men were also simply doing a job.

Publishing the story concerning the crash of Handley Page Hampden I L4054, for example, resulted in the end of a lifelong quest by Maureen Wheelhouse for information as to the fate of her uncle, Aircraftman 1st Class Denis Sharpe, who perished with his fellow crew members near St Mary's Lighthouse on 7th April 1940. The closure felt not only by Maureen but her family, in particular Barbara, Denis's sister, only adds to the satisfaction we feel whilst pursuing this hobby. The pilot and co-pilot of this particular aircraft, Pilot Officer Wilfred Roberts and Pilot Officer Keith Brooke-Taylor, both came from New Zealand and we can only hope that the true story of their fate will travel that far and comfort their relatives.

We feel that the Introduction to this book should include a notice to the public as to the courtesies that should be observed by anyone who wishes to visit crash sites. Many of the sites covered in this book are located on private land and it should be stressed that permission *must* be sought from the landowner, farmer, or other relevant body, before venturing onto the land. Generally speaking, we have found that if we ask politely there is no problem. However, there are other crash sites we have recorded that have quite severe restrictions concerning access. Supermarine Spitfire VA P8563, for example, crashed in what is now designated a Site of Special Scientific Interest as it is home to rare wildlife and flora. In cases such as this, a request for permission to visit a crash site must be made in writing – but it is unlikely that permission will be granted.

Another crash site with limited access is that of Lockheed F-104G Starfighter D-8337, the wreckage of which lies on the Otterburn artillery training ranges. The reasons for paying close attention to one's surroundings in this instance are blatantly obvious. Other sites may contain human remains, so due care and reverence must be observed when visiting them.

Most of the aircraft chronicled in this book were military and in the majority of cases were armed when they crashed. Although the Ministry of Defence cleared each crash site at the time of the accident, live ordnance may still pose a problem, and anything suspicious should remain untouched. Finally, high-ground sites can be especially treacherous and difficult to get to. We advise that only experienced walkers should attempt to approach these crash sites, and never alone.

Introduction

Crash sites involving military aircraft are protected by the Protection of Military Remains Act 1986, and are therefore subject to certain rules and regulations laid down by the government. Remember that these sites are part of our cultural heritage and so their protection is in everyone's interest. It should be noted that it is illegal to disturb or remove any part of an aircraft without the permission of the Ministry of Defence, or the relative country, and that failure to abide by the Act could result in a custodial sentence.

Strict guidelines must be followed when examining crash sites. When approaching the MOD, interested parties must first have positively identified the aircraft in question. It must be proved beyond any doubt that the crew have been recovered and that no ordnance (which generally means bombs) remains on board. For example, it would be difficult to prove beyond doubt that no bombs remain on board a bomber that crashed whilst returning from an operational sortie – and one tends not to be able to hit a bomb with a spade too many times before it goes off! Written permission to examine the site must then be obtained from the landowner.

After all this has been done and accepted and the licence has been granted, the county archaeologist must be approached. He or she will determine whether or not a recovery could damage any local sites of importance, and will have the final say as to whether a recovery can or cannot go ahead.

This then covers what we do and why we do it, the rules that govern our conduct and the laws behind those rules which we must abide by. So enjoy the book and visit the sites, but leave them in the same condition you found them for others to enjoy.

Russell Gray (ACIA)
Jim Corbett (ACIA)
Jonathan Shipley (ACIA)
Neil Anderson (ACIA)
www.acia.co.uk

Map showing locations of the crash sites.

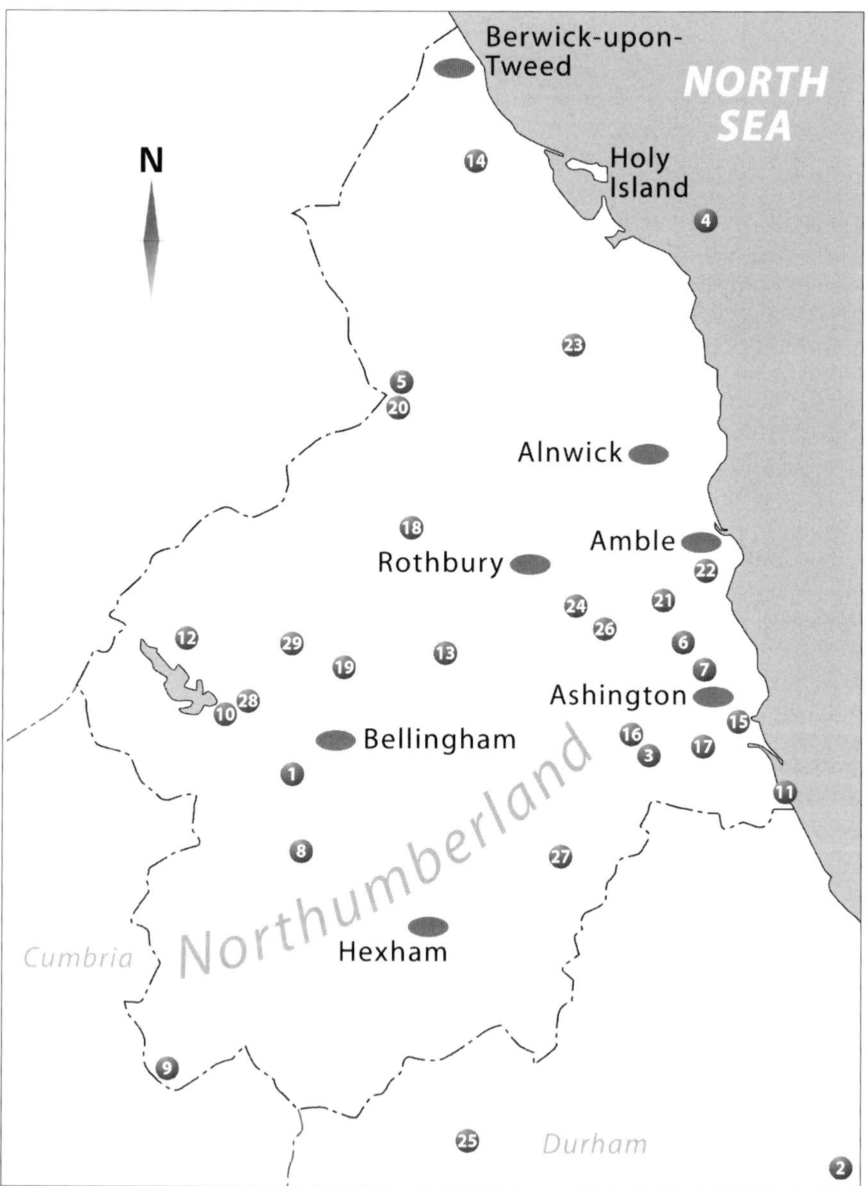

Armstrong Whitworth Whitley V P4952

Aircraft Type:	**Armstrong Whitworth Whitley V**
Serial:	P4952
Code(s):	ZA–R
Unit:	No 10 Squadron, RAF
Base:	RAF Leeming, Yorkshire
Crew:	Pilot: Squadron Leader Kenneth F. Ferguson Bomb Aimer: Sergeant Charles S. Rogers Navigator/Observer: Sergeant Walter Fraser Wireless Operator: Sergeant Ernest Cummings Air Gunner: Sergeant Mark A. Niman
Crash Date:	15th October 1940
Crash Location:	Mesling Crags, three miles south-west of Bellingham, Northumberland
Grid Reference:	80/794822

The Aircraft

Designed in response to Air Ministry Specification B3/34 issued in July 1934, the Whitley twin-engined long-range bomber first flew in prototype form (K4586) on 17th March 1936. Some seven months before this event, in August 1935, the Air Ministry had ordered 80 production Whitleys while it was still in design. This initial order, which was doubled in size in May 1936, comprised 34 Mk Is, 46 Mk IIs and 80 Mk IIIs, with each successive mark powered by a more powerful version of the Armstrong Siddeley Tiger radial engine and, in the case of the Mk III, additional defensive armament in the form of a retractable ventral turret equipped with two .303 calibre machine guns.

By the outbreak of war in September 1939, seven RAF squadrons had re-equipped with Whitleys, 200 of which (160 Mks I–III, 33 Mk IVs and 7 Mk IVAs) had been constructed. The Mk IV and Mk IVA saw a change in power plant as the Tiger radial gave way to the Rolls-Royce Merlin inline. However, full-scale production of the Whitley only commenced with the Mk V, the final bomber variant, 1,466 of which were built before production of this model ceased in June 1943.

The Whitley entered RAF service on 9th March 1937, when the second production Mk I (K7184) was delivered to No 10 Squadron at RAF Dishforth in Yorkshire. The type's operational debut came on 3rd September 1939, when Whitleys of No 51 Squadron and No 58 Squadron carried out a leaflet raid on Bremen, Hamburg and the Ruhr region. Less than two weeks later, on the night of 1st/2nd October, No 10 Squadron's Whitleys became the first RAF bombers to operate over Berlin when they carried out a leaflet raid on the German capital.

Although popular with its crews, the Whitley was a slow and cumbersome aircraft and proved to be easy prey for German fighters and flak batteries. These shortcomings and the arrival of the new generation of four-engined heavy bombers for RAF Bomber Command marked the beginning of the end for the Whitley's career as a front-line bomber, which drew to a close with an attack on Ostend on 29th May 1942. Some training unit examples participated in the '1,000' bomber raid on Cologne the following night, but the vast majority of that force comprised Wellingtons, Halifaxes, Lancasters and Stirlings. Many surviving Whitley Vs were subsequently used as crew trainers and glider tugs, and by 'Special Duties' units involved in dropping secret agents behind enemy lines.

The Crash

Whitley V P4952 took off from RAF Leeming in Yorkshire late in the evening of 15th October 1940 on a mission to bomb the synthetic oil refinery plant at Stettin in Poland. The aircraft had been in service barely six months, having joined No 10 Squadron at RAF Leeming on 9th April 1940 as one of a batch of Mk Vs ordered to replace earlier Mk IVs. Despite atrocious weather conditions the mission was judged a success. However, Stettin was almost at the limit of the Whitley V's operational range, and it was while P4952 was about to cross the English coastline on its return to base that

Crashed 15th October 1940

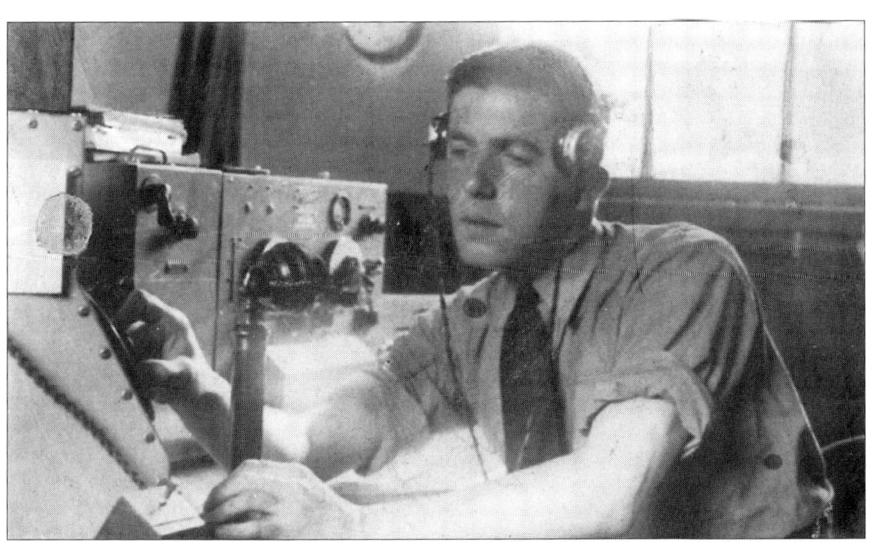

Wireless Operator Ernest Cummings. (P. Cummings)

the crew noticed the aircraft's fuel supply was running low.

As they reached the coast, a message was received from Leeming Air Traffic Control (ATC) informing returning aircraft that the base was fog-bound and that they were all to divert to RAF Marham in Norfolk – an extra 40 miles' flying. Sergeant Ernest Cummings, P4952's wireless operator, contacted Leeming ATC and informed them of the lack of fuel; Leeming ATC responded with instructions for the pilot, Squadron Leader Kenneth Ferguson, to climb to 8,000 feet, point the aircraft in an easterly direction (i.e. out to sea) and for it to be abandoned.

The crew followed the instructions and baled out, but for some unknown reason the aircraft's course had not been altered to point it out to sea. As the five crewmen slowly descended to earth in their parachutes, P4952 hit high ground some three miles south-west of Bellingham in Northumberland. The crew eventually landed some eight miles further south around Ladyhill, near Stonehaugh; they were all fine although a couple of them spent a cold night sleeping in their parachutes.

The Whitley had almost belly-landed on a shallow incline on the northern slopes of Whitchester Moor, near a small rocky outcrop known locally as The Meslings. The front fuselage was crushed on impact, but the rest of the aircraft was reasonably intact when it was discovered by a shepherd from Brieredge the following afternoon. Recovery of the wreckage was a slow process and locals recalled how it was broken up by the farmer and carted down to the roadside at Dunterley, where it remained for a number of weeks until it was taken away on a low-loader.

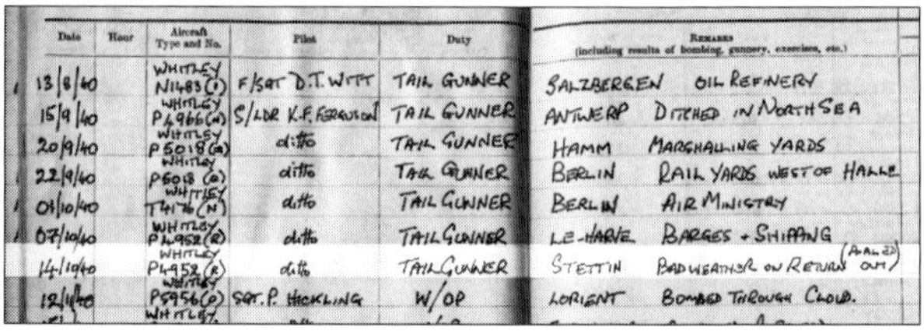

Sgt Mark Niman's logbook showing the incident near Bellingham. **(M. Niman)**

The Aftermath

Almost exactly one month after the crash of P4952, three of her crew members lost their lives when another of No 10 Squadron's Whitleys was lost at sea. Squadron Leader Ferguson, Sergeant Rogers and Sergeant Fraser died when their aircraft, damaged whilst returning from an operation, ditched in the North Sea on 14th November 1940. Despite the best efforts of the search and rescue teams, neither they nor any wreckage of their aircraft were ever found. The names of all three are inscribed on the Runnymede Memorial in Surrey, which commemorates all those who lost their lives during the Second World War whilst serving with the Air Forces of the Commonwealth at bases in Great Britain or in North-western Europe, and who have no known grave.

Sergeant Niman and Sergeant Cummings both survived the war, Niman completing four tours as a wireless operator in various theatres of conflict.

The Crash Site

Some small remains of P4952 can still be located where it came to rest on the open ground. A trail of tiny fragments runs down the hill along the line of the slope the aircraft skidded down before coming to rest in a stream near the bottom. At this point a noticeable depression is evident, caused when the crumpled nose dug into the ground. It was at this point in the early 1980s that members of the North East Aircraft Museum excavated several sections from the nose of P4952, including remains of the wooden crew access ladder.

Jim Corbett

Daniel Corbett accompanied his father on his inspection of the crash site in February 2008. **(J. Corbett)**

Avro Vulcan B2
XM610

Aircraft Type:	**Avro Vulcan B2**
Serial:	XM610
Code(s):	NOT KNOWN
Unit:	No 44 Squadron, RAF
Base:	RAF Waddington, Lincolnshire
Crew:	Pilot: Flight Lieutenant Garth Robert 'Bob' Alcock Co-pilot: Flying Officer Peter Hoskins Navigator Plotter: Flight Lieutenant James 'Jim' Vinales Navigator Radar: Flying Officer Roger Barker Air Electronics Officer: Flight Lieutenant James Power
Crash Date:	8th January 1971
Crash Location:	Trimdon, County Durham
Grid Reference:	93/408366

The Aircraft

In 1945/6, at the dawn of the atomic age, the Air Staff formulated a requirement for new bombers to equip RAF Bomber Command. This led to Specification B35/46, issued on 1st July 1947, which required Great Britain's aircraft manufacturers to submit designs for bombers powered by four jet engines and capable of carrying heavy payloads for long distances at great subsonic speeds and at high altitudes.

The challenging combination of requirements led to some radical and innovative designs, nowhere more so than in the wing configurations.

Avro Vulcan B2 XM610

Crashed 8th January 1971

Avro chose a delta plan-form for its Avro 698 which was accepted for development in November 1947, followed in early 1949 by an order for two prototypes of what became the world's first large delta-wing bomber.

The prototype Avro 698 (VX770) first flew on 30th August 1952 powered

Vulcan B2 – XL319. **(North East Aircraft Museum))**

by four Rolls Royce RA3 Avon turbojets, but was re-engined with Armstrong Siddeley Sapphire turbojets after 32 flying hours. The second prototype (VX777) joined the flight-test programme on 3rd September 1953 and acted as test-bed for the much more powerful Bristol Olympus 101 turbojet. The Olympus was selected to power the production aircraft, christened Vulcan in late 1952, 45 of which were ordered. Both prototypes sported the original delta-wing with straight wing leading-edge, as did the first production Vulcan B1 (XA889) when it roared into the sky on 4th February 1955. A pressurised cabin housed the five-man crew, three of whom sat behind the pilot and co-pilot, at a lower level and facing rearwards.

The Vulcan B1 eventually entered service with RAF Bomber Command on 20th July 1956, early examples going to No 230 Operational Conversion Unit (OCU); but it was not until 11th July 1957 that No 83 Squadron, also based at RAF Waddington, became the first of six squadrons to receive the new bomber. Later-production aircraft had a revised wing configuration to counter handling problems associated with the significant increase in engine thrust offered by the Olympus engine.

Even before the Vulcan B1 entered service, Avro was working on the design of a larger wing for the next production model: the Vulcan B2. The new model, 89 of which were ordered, entered service with No 230 OCU on 1st July 1960 and was assigned to nine squadrons. An increase in wing area and greater engine power (from Olympus 201/301s) enabled it to fly faster, higher and further with a heavier payload that included the Blue Steel thermonuclear missile.

When the Royal Navy took over the strategic deterrence role with its Polaris submarines in the late 1960s, the RAF's Vulcan force adopted a tactical role, penetrating at low level armed with up to 21,000 pounds of free-fall bombs; and it was in this role that a Vulcan B2 (XM597) bombed the airfield at Port Stanley during the Falklands War in 1982 on the first 'Black Buck' raid. By then the Vulcan force was already being retired from service, but six Vulcan K2s soldiered on with No 50 Squadron as air tankers until they – the last Vulcans in service – were retired in 1984.

The Crash

On 7th January 1971 a No 44 Squadron crew was tasked to fly a Hi–Lo–Hi training mission over the border counties of England. Their aircraft was to be Vulcan B2 XM610 of the Waddington Wing. The first part of the mission went well and the Vulcan descended from high level off the Northumberland coast and entered the North of England low-flying zone, taking the aircraft through the Northern Pennines and Cheviot Hills. Halfway through the low-level part of the mission, XM610 was cruising at 300 knots on 75 per cent power at 500 feet over the hills near Kelso. At the controls, Flight Lieutenant Bob Alcock could see that the weather ahead was rapidly deteriorating, so he decided to abandon the rest of the low-level flying and climb back to a safe altitude.

Having informed the rest of the crew of what he was about to do, Alcock increased the power to 85 per cent, raised the nose and started to climb away. A few seconds later there was a loud explosion and the Vulcan slewed to the left. Alcock scanned his instruments and noticed that the RPMs on No 1 engine were running down and the jet pipe temperature was rapidly rising to its limit; then the fire-warning light for No 1 engine lit up. Alcock informed the crew of the situation, shut the high-pressure cock and closed the throttle. Next he pressed the 'Fire' button and closed the 'Engine Air' switch. While Alcock was carrying out these tasks, Flight Lieutenant Jim Power, the Air Electronics Officer, confirmed that there was alternator failure on No 1 engine and switched off and isolated the alternator. He then used the Vulcan's rear-facing periscope to scan the aircraft and informed Alcock that he could see damage to the airframe in the area of the rear of No 1 engine.

***Standing in the line of the crash site in June 2008.* (R. Gray)**

The fire-warning light went out as Alcock continued his climb on three engines, and the fire-warning system was checked to ensure it was still operating. Running his eyes over the instruments again, Alcock noticed that the jet pipe temperature on No 2 engine was now rising, and shortly afterwards the engine's fire-warning light came on. He shouted another warning to the crew, then grabbed the Ram Air Turbine release handle to let the turbine swing down into the slipstream; in doing this, all non-essential electrical loads were shed from the aircraft's electrical bus bars.

The cockpit lit up like a Christmas tree as warning lights blinked on all over the instrument panels. No 2 engine was shut down in the same manner as No 1, requiring Alcock to use a lot of left boot to keep the aircraft straight. The 'Fire' button for No 2 engine was pressed and after a few seconds the fire-warning light went out.

Taking stock of what had happened, Alcock asked Power to read out the emergency procedures from the flight reference cards. Whilst doing so, Power again scanned the undersurface of the Vulcan with the rear-facing periscope, but everything still looked the same. Alcock reached over to the centre instrument console and pushed the rudder trim switch to take the pressure off his left foot. It was now time to declare an in-flight emergency, so a Mayday call was transmitted. Flight Lieutenant Jim Vinales, in his role as Navigator Plotter, passed an accurate plot of their position to Alcock, this information to be transmitted with the Mayday call.

Flying Officer Peter Hoskins, the co-pilot, was 'playing tunes' on the fuel console as he opened the cross-feed cocks and transferred fuel from the port-side fuel tanks in an attempt to keep the Vulcan's centre of gravity within acceptable limits. Meanwhile, Jim Power had used the cartridge-start system to fire up the Aircraft Auxiliary Power Unit to provide more electrical power, and was in the process of gradually restoring selected aircraft systems to life. Half of the power flying controls (PFC) had been shed in the emergency, and these were restarted with the exception of the auxiliary rudder PFC.

Jim Power was very busy running through the Vulcan's flight reference cards and doing his switching when he noticed a glow in the eyepiece of the periscope. Taking a closer look, Power got a very nasty shock when he saw that the glow was the result of a fire raging in the area of No 1 engine. Just as Power shouted a warning, the fire-warning light for No 2 engine re-lit again and remained lit for two minutes. The Mayday call was transmitted again and Alcock gave orders to the three crew members in the rear cockpit: 'Put on parachutes and prepare to bale out'.

As XM610 was now in cloud, Alcock delayed the order to jump until the Vulcan entered clear skies near Rothbury, at an altitude of 6,000 feet. The crew set the Identification Friend or Foe system to emergency and donned their parachutes. Static lines and emergency oxygen were connected, masks were put on and toggles were turned down. Life rafts and personal survival packs (PSP) were connected to their lanyards. Protective helmets were donned and tightened down. Flying Officer Roger Barker, Navigator Radar, was now down by the crew door situated on the floor. Jim Vinales pulled the cabin depressurization handle and one by one the crew called 'Ready'.

Just ten minutes after the first explosion in No 1 engine, Bob Alcock gave the order, 'Static line manual override. Jump! Jump!' The three crewmen in the rear cockpit pulled their emergency oxygen knobs; down by the door, Roger Barker grasped the door-opening handle, moved it outboard then straight through to the emergency position. With a very loud roar the door opened and dust flew into the rear cockpit as the slipstream hurtled by at 200 knots. Barker sat on the sill at the top of the door, pulled his knees up to his chest, put his arms around his knees and clasped his hands together to keep himself in a tight ball. Hitching up his PSP and dinghy over the sill, he slid down the door. As the underside of the aircraft whipped past, he felt the static line jerk at his parachute; his hand flew to the manual handle and yanked it. With a loud crack the parachute opened and he was instantly struck by the sudden silence.

Jim Power followed Barker out and Jim Vinales was the last of the three to leave the rear cockpit. All three made a safe descent and landed in fields near Rothbury. After landing, all three activated their search and rescue beacon equipment. Within a few minutes a Whirlwind helicopter from No 202 Squadron at RAF Boulmer in Northumberland was homing onto them.

Bob Alcock decided to try to nurse XM610 back to the master diversion airfield at RAF Leeming in Yorkshire, helped by co-pilot Peter Hoskins. The fate of XM610, however, had been sealed from the moment of the first explosion – nothing the crew did from that moment onwards could have saved the aircraft. After trying a few handling manoeuvres, Alcock tested XM610's low-speed handling, but broke off at 185 knots as the aircraft became difficult to control. Ahead lay the Tyneside conurbation, so Alcock nursed the bomber overhead at 6,000 feet, trying to steer clear of the built-up area.

As Sunderland slipped by on the port side, Alcock slowly turned XM610, by now blazing fiercely, out towards the sea. Thousands of people on the ground watched as the crippled Vulcan passed over, pieces of debris falling from the port wing and engines. Near Easington, Alcock ordered 'Jettison canopy'. He and Hoskins reached for their jettison levers and pulled them back. A loud bang just behind their heads confirmed that the jettison gun had fired and the canopy was whipped away from above their heads. Alcock could now see the full extent of the fire over his left shoulder and he did not like what he saw.

The noise in the cockpit after the canopy was jettisoned made all verbal communication impossible, so Alcock jerked his right thumb up in a sign for Hoskins to initiate ejection from the aircraft. Hoskins reached for his seat pan handle, straightened his back, braced himself and then yanked the handle. There was a one-second delay, then with a double bang Hoskins' ejection seat fired. His feet were yanked off the rudder pedals as his legs were pulled back and secured to the ejection seat as it accelerated up the rail, reaching a maximum speed of 60 feet per second.

As the coastline passed beneath the Vulcan's nose, Alcock took one last look around; then he too pulled his seat pan firing handle. Just 1½ seconds after the seat fired, Alcock was 80 feet clear of the aircraft. The drogue gun on the ejection seat fired, pulling out the drogue parachute to stabilize the seat. Another 1½ seconds and the barostat operated, releasing the harness and leg restraints and allowing Alcock to fall from the ejection seat. The pull of the drogue parachute was transferred from the ejection seat to his main parachute, hauling it out of its pack and allowing it to open and start a safe descent with Alcock attached.

With no one at the controls, XM610 entered a downwards spiral. Instead of crashing into the sea the Vulcan dived into a field behind the old Co-op store at Station Town, near Wingate in County Durham. The resulting explosion completely destroyed the aircraft and left a large crater. Luckily, no one on the ground was hurt; but if XM610 had crashed 100 yards either side, there would have been heavy loss of life.

The Aftermath

The inquiry into the crash of XM610 traced the cause to fatigue failure of a high-pressure turbine blade in No 1 engine. The blade became jammed in the periphery of the turbine disc and rotated with it, finally causing the casing to rupture. The turbine then broke up, causing high-speed debris to pierce the engine casing and engine bay walls, damaging No 2 engine and the outboard No 3 and No 4 wing fuel tanks. The flames continued to spread out of control, fed by fuel from the damaged tanks. By the time Alcock ejected, XM610 was in danger of breaking up, with pieces already falling away and the flames spreading along the wing.

Soon after the crash, all of the RAF's Vulcans were fitted with titanium armour plates in the engine bays, in the area of the high-pressure turbines, and also in the roof of the bomb bay. This plating was designed to prevent debris from any exploding engine damaging the next engine, entering the bomb bay or rupturing the fuel tanks and causing the loss of the aircraft.

Flight Lieutenant Alcock was awarded the Air Force Cross for his valiant efforts to save his aircraft. In addition, Alcock was RAF Man of the Year for 1971. The rest of the crew each received the Queen's Commendation for Valuable Service in the Air.

The Crash Site

This crash site is well worth a visit although, as with all lowland crash sites, there is little or no visible surface debris. That being said, however, the last time I visited this site in June 2008 it only took me five minutes to stumble across a fragment of the aircraft. The impact area is in the middle of the field next to a drain and adjacent to a small burn which runs through the field. The field is overlooked on two sides by some relatively new houses. In fact, while I was taking photographs, a friendly local came across and showed me where one of the engines had impacted and which is apparently still there but some thirty feet underground.

At the time of writing, the site is very much accessible so long as you remember to close the gate and not let the horses out but, as always, permission should be sought. As you stand in the field it is difficult not to contemplate what could have happened had the Vulcan crashed some 500 yards sooner; the consequences of this would have been catastrophic and the loss of life substantial. Indeed, the locals maintain that the aircraft was on course to crash sooner but by some miracle it seemed to 'float' over the final row of houses only to crash harmlessly in the empty field. I think it is fair to say that luck was very much on the side of Trimdon's community that day.

Russell Gray and Jim Rutland

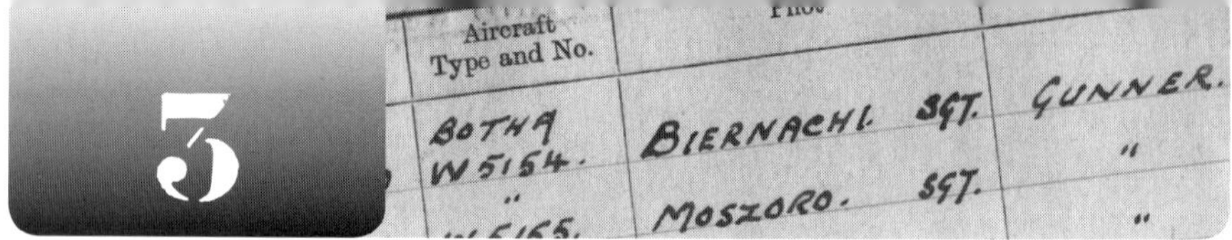

Blackburn Botha Is W5137 and W5154

Aircraft Type:	**Blackburn Botha I**
Serials:	W5137 and W5154
Code(s):	14 and 10
Unit:	No 4 Air Gunnery School, RAF
Base:	RAF Morpeth, Northumberland
Crew (W5137):	Pilot: Pilot Officer G. R. Jackson Air Gunner: Sergeant E. Hall Trainee: Leading Aircraftman A. W. van Egmond Trainee: Aircraftman 2nd Class B. E. van Opdorp Trainee: Aircraftman 2nd Class R. van den Bron
Crew (W5154):	Pilot: Flight Lieutenant S. Z. Zarski Air Gunner: Leading Aircraftman F. L. Beresford Trainee: Leading Aircraftman D. J. Kooij Trainee: Leading Aircraftman F. van Westenbrugge
Crash Date:	29th March 1943
Crash Location:	RAF Morpeth, Northumberland
Grid Reference:	81/186825

The Aircraft

Originally designed in 1936 to Air Ministry Specification M15/35, which called for a three-man general reconnaissance/torpedo bomber powered by two Bristol Perseus engines, the Blackburn Botha proved to be

Crashed 29th March 1943

***The Bristol Botha, a rather unsuccessful aircraft that was used for training Air Gunners at 4 Air Gunner School RAF Morpeth.* (J. Shipley)**

something of a failure. Initially it was thought to be a better design than the Bristol Beaufort (see Chapter 7), with which it was in direct competition as a torpedo bomber, and this was reflected in an order for 442 Botha Is straight off the drawing board compared to only 78 Beaufort Is.

A change in the requirement to a crew of four raised the weights of both aircraft, which led to a plan to use more powerful Bristol Taurus engines. However, a shortage of these engines meant that they were supplied for Beauforts only, leaving the Botha to be fitted with the underpowered Bristol Perseus.

The first Botha (L6104) conducted its maiden flight on 28th December 1938, and handling problems and a serious lack of power were immediately apparent. Modifications were made to the airframe, and on 12th December 1939 the RAF received its first production Botha I. The original plan called for the Botha to form part of RAF Coastal Command's pre-war re-equipment programme, but in the event it was not until June 1940 that large numbers were taken on strength when No 1 Operational Training Unit (OTU) received 25 examples with which to train crews.

The Botha's operational career was restricted to service with just one operational unit, No 608 (North Riding) Squadron at RAF Thornaby in

		Type and No.		
24·6·42	11·40	BOTHA W 5154.	BIERNACHI. SGT.	GUNNER.
30·6·42	20·00	" W 5155.	MOSZORO. SGT.	"
4·7·42	08·00	" W 5119.	BIENIASZ SGT.	"
4·7·42	11·55	" W 5089	JEDLICKO SGT.	"
7·7·42	10·55	" W 5138	RESKO SGT.	"
11·7·42	07·15	" L 6510	GARSTECKI SGT.	"
11·7·42	12·15	L 6510	SWITALSKI SGT.	"
11·7·42	19·55	" W 5052	JAWORSKI SGT.	"
13·7·42	16·25	" W 5052	ILOTT SGT.	"
19·7·42	07·05	" W 5124	JEDLICKO SGT.	"
19·7·42	12·00	" W 5137	GEBHARD SGT.	"
21·7·42	11·15	" W 5139	MOSZORO SGT.	"
21·7·42	15·55	" W 5119	SWITALSKI SGT.	"
22·7·42	07·55	" W 5156	BIENIAZS. SGT.	"
		TOTAL FLYING HOURS		· 13 HRS · 30MIN

A page from the Air Gunners Log Book of F/Lt R. R. Shipley.

(including results of bombing, gunnery, exercises, etc.)	Day	Night
AIR TO SEA, BUOYS. (NO ROUNDS FIRED).	·40	
AIR TO AIR, BEAM. (NO ROUNDS FIRED).	1·05	
AIR TO AIR, BEAM (200 ROUNDS).	1·30	
AIR TO AIR, BEAM (100 ROUNDS).	1·20	
AIR TO AIR, AIRCRAFT U/S. NO ROUNDS FIRED.	·10	
AIR TO AIR, UNDERTAIL. (100 ROUNDS).	1·20	
AIR TO AIR, UNDERTAIL. NO LYSANDER.	·55	
AIR TO AIR, UNDERTAIL. (200 ROUNDS).	1·00	
AIR TO AIR. UNDERTAIL. (200 ROUNDS)	·35	
AIR TO AIR. OBSERVATION OF TRACER. – (200 ROUNDS)	·55	
AIR TO AIR OBSERVATION OF TRACER – (200 ROUNDS).	01·00	
AIR TO AIR (TRACER). UNDERTAIL. (200 ROUNDS)	·55	
AIR TO AIR (TRACER). UNDERTAIL (200 ROUNDS)	01·15	
AIR TO AIR (TRACER) BEAM, APPARENT RELATIVE SPEED. (NO TARGET)	·50	
[signature] S/LDR. CHIEF INSTRUCTOR. No 4. A.G.S. MORPETH.		

Yorkshire, which used the type to conduct patrols over the North Sea from 10th August 1940; but a series of unexplained fatal accidents and the type's inferior performance, even with a more powerful version of the Perseus engine, led to its withdrawal from front-line service on 6th November 1940 after a total of 308 patrols.

Training units received the vast majority of the 580 Botha Is built, one such being No 4 Air Gunnery School (AGS), formed at RAF Morpeth in Northumberland in March 1942. The first Botha I was due to be taken on strength at No 4 AGS on 11th April 1942, but the aircraft crashed near RAF Ouston during its delivery flight, injuring the pilot, Flying Officer Preston. It was not until the following day that the unit received its first two Bothas in the shape of W5133 and W5146, both of which landed safely. Five days later, on 17th April, No 4 AGS was officially opened. RAF Morpeth had at last become a flying unit.

By the end of May 1942, No 1 Course was under way, the initial intake of 45 trainee airmen having arrived two days earlier. Their ground training commenced on the 25th, by which time they had already witnessed the loss of one Botha I when W5146 crashed on the airfield prior to take-off – the fourth aircraft to be damaged in a flying accident since the arrival of the first Bothas just six weeks earlier. By the time the trainees started aerial training on 31st May, yet another aircraft, a Westland Lysander target tug (P2575), had crashed, this time on landing. The Bothas, each of which featured a pair of .303 calibre machine guns in a power-operated dorsal turret and a single fixed forward-firing .303 in the nose, carried the trainee air gunners who then fired at ground targets near Druridge Bay to the east, or at drogues towed by the Lysanders, again over the sea near Druridge.

On 4th July 1942 No 1 Course passed out, all of its pupils having successfully completed the training course. These newly qualified air gunners were then sent on to OTUs where they became part of bomber crews prior to joining operational squadrons in RAF Bomber Command. During the month it had taken No 1 Course to complete its training, three more groups of trainees had been posted to No 4 AGS and had commenced training, giving some idea of the numbers of airmen passing through the station. This system of training continued throughout 1942, although early experience led to a slight lengthening of the course.

In February 1943, No 24 Course arrived at RAF Morpeth and commenced training on the 21st of the month. Within this group were a large number of Dutch naval cadets who, according to the end-of-course report, 'had worked extremely hard in overcoming the language handicap'. Just six out of the 60 trainees who started No 24 Course failed to finish.

The Crash

On 29th March, just over a week before No 24 Course was due to pass out, RAF Morpeth was visited by Air Marshal Sir Philip Babington. At about 10.35 hours, Botha I W5154 flown by Flight Lieutenant Zarski took off on gunnery detail. On board with him were Beresford, Kooij and van Westenbrugge. Like many of the pilots based at RAF Morpeth, Zarski was Polish and had

The view across a dispersal bay to a lone hangar surviving at RAF Morpeth. (J. Shipley)

previously served in the Polish Air Force before making his way to Great Britain. He was an experienced pilot who had amassed some 2,128 flying hours, 1,700 of which were with the Polish Air Force. He appears to have been amongst the original pilots to join No 4 AGS and is noted in the unit's Operational Records Book (ORB) as having been the most senior Polish officer at RAF Morpeth, with 361 flying hours on the Botha.

With the training exercise finished, Zarski returned to base at about 11.40 hours, having been airborne for just over an hour. As the aircraft neared home, Pilot Officer Jackson took off in Botha I W5137 on another gunnery exercise with Hall, van Egmond, van Opdorp and van den Bron on board. Born in Auckland in New Zealand on 28th January 1921, Jackson had been awarded his pilot's badge on 4th October 1941. He joined No 4 AGS on 18th April 1942 and was, like Flight Lieutenant Zarski, one of the original pilots to be posted to the unit. By the time he took off on 29th March, Jackson had some 217 flying hours on the Botha, along with some 243 hours on other aircraft.

Although not referred to a great deal in the ORB, it would appear that Jackson had been involved in a minor mishap on 1st October 1942, when the Botha he was piloting left the runway and sank into mud causing some damage to the undercarriage. This kind of incident seems to have been rather common at the station, but compared to the many fatal accidents that occurred during the first year of flying, both Jackson and Zarski had managed to emerge relatively unscathed. This, however, was all about to change.

Jackson's Botha had just taken to the air and was in the circuit at about 1,200 feet when the Botha flown by Zarski entered the circuit and attempted to land. Official documents state that it would appear both pilots made a last-minute attempt to avoid a collision, but that their efforts were unsuccessful. At 11.45 hours the two Bothas collided in mid-air about two miles to the east of RAF Morpeth, near the RAF site at Stannington. All nine airmen aboard the two aircraft were killed.

The exact cause of the collision is not known, but RAF Morpeth seems to have lacked any real watch tower and air traffic control facilities. There has also been a suggestion that the weather on the day may have contributed to the accident. Saul Muller, a Belgian who was training as an air gunner as part of the Dutch Navy contingent of No 24 Course, recalled in a local newspaper that the skies were particularly cloudy on the morning of the crash, but that No 4 AGS had nevertheless been encouraged to put up a few aircraft to show training in progress when Air Marshal Sir Philip Babington visited. Although the unit's ORB and the Form 1180 (Loss Card) for the two Bothas does not mention the weather conditions, dense low cloud could have hampered visibility if it had not cleared, and could have increased the likelihood of an accident.

The Aftermath

On 2nd April 1943 the body of Flight Lieutenant Zarski was laid to rest in the churchyard in Morpeth. The following day, during a military funeral held at 15.00 hours at the same cemetery, the bodies of Jackson, Beresford, Kooij, van Westenbrugge, van Opdorp, van Egmond and van den Bron were also laid to rest. The body of Sergeant Edward Hall was taken to Edinburgh Eastern Cemetery where it was interred.

The Crash Site

The official documents (i.e. the aircraft Loss Card and the Station ORB) are very sketchy about the location of the site, simply stating that it is near the airfield or near RAF Stannington.

From this information it would appear that the aircraft wreckage fell in an area that is now used for arable farming, although such a mid-air collision and the break-up that clearly followed would result in wreckage being scattered over quite an area. The area covered by the grid reference given seems to be the most likely site where the two Botha aircraft came down, although no wreckage has been located to positively identify it. One has to remember that a low-ground site on land that was (and still is) very easily accessed by machinery would have been thoroughly cleared by the salvage team; however, the search for fragments to positively identify the site, or for an eyewitness, continues.

Although the location of the final resting place of Bothas W5137 and W5154 has not been found (as yet), the most important reminder has to be the graves of the nine airmen who died in the skies of Northumberland. It is these graves, like so many others throughout the British Isles, that are the true lasting reminders of the many brave men and women who made the ultimate sacrifice.

Jonathan Shipley

4

Boeing B-17F-80BO Flying Fortress 42-30030

Aircraft Type:	**Boeing B-17F-80BO Flying Fortress**
Serial:	42-30030
Code(s):	A
Unit:	560th Bomb Squadron, 388th Bomb Group, USAAF
Base:	Knettishall (Station 136), Norfolk
Crew:	Pilot: Lieutenant Henry J. Nagorka Co-pilot: 2nd Lieutenant Gilbert N. Parker Navigator: 2nd Lieutenant John B. Leverone Bombardier: 2nd Lieutenant Michael G. Mahoney Flight Engineer: Technical Sergeant Edward E. Keisler Radio Operator: Technical Sergeant Francis J. Antalek Ball Gunner: Staff Sergeant Robert A. Blankenburg Waist Gunner: Staff Sergeant Edward G. Christensen Waist Gunner: Staff Sergeant Claude E. Whitehead Tail Gunner: Staff Sergeant Jack S. Harris
Crash Date:	17th September 1943
Crash Location:	Near the Farne Islands, Seahouses, Northumberland
Grid Reference:	N/A

Boeing B-17F-80BO Flying Fortress 42-30030

Crashed 17th September 1943

The Aircraft

In the same way that the Avro Lancaster is synonymous with the RAF's bombing campaign during the Second World War, so the aerial armadas of Boeing B-17 Flying Fortresses have come to epitomise the crucial part played by the United States Army Air Forces (USAAF) in the bombing campaign against Hitler's 'Fortress Europe'. Yet the B-17 was designed to meet a US Army Air Corps (USAAC) requirement, issued in May 1934, for a multi-engined bomber whose role would be to defend the United States through high-altitude bombing of invasion fleets at sea. It had to be able to carry a bomb load of 2,000 pounds at least 1,020 miles, at a speed of 200 mph (but 250 mph if possible). Prototypes were to be ready by August 1935 for Army trials.

Boeing's response to the challenge drew on the experience it had gained with the design and construction of the Model 294 (XB-15) long-range bomber. The result was the Model 299: a four-engined bomber that could carry 4,800 pounds of bombs and defend itself with machine guns in the nose and four fuselage blisters aft of the wing. The prototype (X13372) took to the air on 28th July 1935 and later flew non-stop from Seattle to Wright Field in Ohio for the trials – a distance of 2,100 miles – in nine hours, thus surpassing the performance requirements.

The Model 299 was subsequently written off during the trials programme, but the bomber's potential was evident and led to an order for thirteen YB-17s (later Y1B-17) for Service tests. These were the first examples to be powered by Wright Cyclone GR-1820 radial engines; and the addition of turbo-superchargers to the engines on one of these aircraft gave it a top speed of 311 mph above 30,000 feet.

The first production model, the B-17B, flew on 27th June 1939. Thirty-nine were built and featured a larger rudder and flaps and a modified nose for the bomb aimer (one of a crew of nine). This was followed by the B-17C (38 built) with upgraded engines and revised defensive armament, some of which were later upgraded to B-17D standard (42 built) in which the external bomb racks were deleted, self-sealing fuel tanks were added and provision was made for a tenth crewman. Operational experience with the D-model led in turn to the B-17E (512 built) with enlarged tail surfaces to improve stability, and completely revised defensive armament that included a tail turret.

With the United States' entry into the war in Europe came the deployment of the Eighth Air Force and the B-17E, the first of which arrived in July 1942 for the 92nd Bomb Group. These went into action on 17th August 1942, by which time the first B-17F (41-24340) was undergoing trials, having flown for the first time on 30th May 1942.

Although externally very similar to the E-model, the B-17F could be distinguished by a one-piece Plexiglas nose cone that replaced the previous framed nose. Other improvements as a direct result of combat experience in the Pacific included the refitting of external bomb racks to increase the bomb load to 20,800 pounds, improved armour protection for the crew, increased fuel capacity and more powerful engines. Defensive armament comprised twelve .30 and .50 calibre machine guns in the nose, radio compartment, mid-upper turret, two waist stations, ventral (ball) turret and tail turret.

B-17 42-30030 – 'Old Ironsides' seen at Knettishall, prior to its crash near Seahouses. (M. Antalek)

The B-17F was also the first model to be ordered in large numbers: 3,405 were built by Boeing (2,300), Douglas (605) and Lockheed (500); and it formed the backbone of the Eighth Air Force – the 'Mighty Eighth' – in Great Britain until the arrival of the B-17G (see Chapter 5) in late-1943. Operations conducted by B-17Fs included the first USAAF attack on Germany itself when Wilhelmshaven was bombed on 27th January 1943.

One of the Eighth Air Force units to receive B-17Fs was the 546th Bomb Squadron, 384th Bomb Group based at Grafton Underwood (Station 107) in Northamptonshire, to which B-17F-80BO 42-30030 was assigned on 1st April 1943. Whilst with this unit it flew a total of seven missions before damage sustained on 29th July 1943 forced the aircraft out of service for repair. Once repaired it was transferred to the 560th Bomb Squadron, 388th Bomb Group based at Knettishall (Station 136) in Norfolk, which had undertaken its first mission on 17th July 1943. Before long the new bomber was nicknamed *Old Ironsides* by her crew.

The Crash

At 11.41 hours on 16th September 1943 *Old Ironsides* took off from Knettishall on a mission to bomb the submarine pens at Bordeaux in France. In all, 21 B-17Fs from the 384th Bomb Group were scheduled to participate, but this was reduced to sixteen because of difficulties experienced by the ground crews in fuelling five of the aircraft prior to the mission. After the bombers had formed up over the North Sea, the briefed route was followed to Bordeaux, where the primary and secondary targets were found to be obscured by cloud. An alternative target was selected further up the coast at La Pallice where the force dropped its bombs. Opposition from enemy fighters was very light.

On the return journey the crew of *Old Ironsides* encountered problems with their radio, and eventually became lost. Several hours later, after flying around in an unsuccessful attempt to find land, *Old Ironsides* ran out of fuel and at around 00.25 hours on 17th September, ditched in the sea close to the Farne Islands off the Northumberland coast.

The ditching was witnessed by a local fisherman who immediately informed the Coast Guard station at North Sunderland and Holy Island. On arriving at the scene they found eight of the crew huddled together on the rocks, one of them, Staff Sergeant Harris, having suffered a broken

Some of the crew of B-17 42-30030 – kneeling in front row (left to right) Jack S. Harris (lost leg in ditching), S/Sgt Claude E. Whitehead (killed in ditching), T/Sgt Francis J. Antalek, S/Sgt Robert A. Blankenburg, S/Sgt Edward G. Christensen (killed in ditching) and T/Sgt Edward E. Keisler. Standing in back row (left to right) Lt Lester Baum (not involved in ditching), Lt Francis E. Tierney (not involved in ditching), 2nd Lt Gilbert N. Parker, and Lt Henry J. Nagorka. **(M. Antalek)**

leg in the ditching. Eight crew members had managed to leave the aircraft with their dinghies just before it broke in two and sank. Sadly, the two waist gunners went down with the aircraft and were drowned. The coast guard, who had first aid experience, put Sergeant Harris's broken leg in splints and used one of the dinghies as a makeshift stretcher to carry him across the rocky ground to the waiting lifeboat.

The eight survivors arrived at North Sunderland lifeboat station at around 02.45 hours. Some time later, and despite the best efforts of a doctor, Staff Sergeant Harris's leg was found to be so badly injured that it had to be amputated. Two weeks after the crash, Staff Sergeant Whitehead's body was washed ashore. The body of Staff Sergeant Christensen was never recovered and is still in the remains of his aircraft.

T/Sgt Francis J. Antalek.
(M. Antalek)

The Aftermath

Just over three weeks after the loss of *Old Ironsides*, on 9th October 1943, seven of the eight surviving crew members were involved in another crash, this time off the coast of Denmark. Returning from a mission to Gydnia in Poland in B-17G *Iza Angel II* (see opposite), their aircraft was attacked and set alight by Luftwaffe Messerschmitt Bf109 fighters. Six of the crew managed to bale out before *Iza Angel II* plummeted into the sea.

Of those who survived the ditching of *Old Ironsides* at Seahouses, fortune again smiled on pilot Lieutenant Nagorka, Technical Sergeant Antalek, 2nd Lieutenant Leverone and 2nd Lieutenant Mahoney, all of whom were rescued and became prisoners of war. Technical Sergeant Blankenburg, Technical Sergeant Keisler and 2nd Lieutenant Parker were all killed. The bodies of Blankenburg and Keisler were later washed ashore; that of Harris was never found.

The Crash Site

Although *Old Ironsides* ditched some distance out to sea, over the years some remains of the aircraft have been dragged nearer to the shore, having been caught in fishing nets. These remains, which include an engine and part of the main wing spar, are visible at very rare and extremely low tides in an area known as the Black Rocks.

Jim Corbett

5

Boeing B-17G-55DL Flying Fortress 44-6504

Aircraft Type:	**Boeing B-17G-55DL Flying Fortress**
Serial:	44-6504
Code(s):	PU–M
Unit:	360th Bomb Squadron, 303rd Bomb Group, USAAF
Base:	Molesworth (Station 107), Cambridgeshire
Crew:	Pilot: 2nd Lieutenant George A. Kyle Co-pilot: Flying Officer James H. Hardy Navigator: Flying Officer Fred Holcombe Bomb aimer: Sergeant Frank R. Turner Radio Operator: Sergeant Joel A. Berly Flight Engineer: Sergeant Ernest G. Schieferstein Waist Gunner: Sergeant William R. Kaufmann Ball Gunner: Sergeant George P. Smith Tail Gunner: Sergeant Howard F. Delaney
Crash Date:	16th December 1944
Crash Location:	Braydon Crag, West Hill, The Cheviot, Northumberland
Grid Reference:	74/894213

The Aircraft

Just as improvements found in the B-17F (see Chapter 4) were a response to operational experience with the B-17E in the Pacific, so the B-17G sought to address shortcomings in the B-17F that were highlighted after the Eighth Air Force commenced operations over Germany on 27th January 1943. As the campaign grew during the year, the Luftwaffe responded by bolstering its air defence units until, by the summer, a force of some 800 fighters flown by many experienced pilots drawn from other operational fronts awaited the bombers.

The B-17F was popular with Eighth Air Force crews and had the reputation of being able to sustain considerable damage and still make it home. However, when the Bomb Groups undertook a series of raids against targets in Germany from August to October 1943, the marauding Luftwaffe fighters cruelly exposed the B-17F's vulnerability to head-on attack.

The response from Boeing was the B-17G, the most obvious feature of which was a Bendix twin-gun 'chin' turret positioned beneath the nose and armed with two .50 calibre machine guns. The new model could also fly higher than any of the previous B-17s – up to 35,000 feet – thanks to the addition of a turbo-supercharger on each engine.

The B-17G also proved to be the most numerous variant, with 8,680 built by Boeing, Douglas and Lockheed. One of the Douglas-built examples

The crew of 44-6504. Top row, left to right, Kyle, Hardy, Holcombe, Corzeskiewiesz (removed from crew shortly after this picture was taken) and Schwieferstein. Front row, left to right, Turner, Berly, Kaufmann, Delaney and Smith. **(Carol Kyle Sage)**

that rolled off the Long Beach line was B-17G-55DL 44-6504, which was added to the USAAF inventory on 24th August 1944 and arrived in Great Britain on 16th September that year. Thirteen days later, 44-6504 was flown to Molesworth in Cambridgeshire (Station 107) to join the 360th Bomb Squadron, 303rd Bomb Group.

By the time 44-6504 sat at dispersal early on the morning of 19th October, armed and ready for a mission to Mannheim, it had already taken part in six missions. Nearby the ball gunner of B-17G-55DL 44-6517, Corporal Harvey N. Kaber, was having difficulty loading his guns. Not realising that the ammunition had slipped back into the feed chute, Kaber test-fired the guns, discharging five rounds into the starboard wing of 44-6504. Almost immediately the bomber caught fire, but fire tenders were on the scene within two minutes and managed to control the blaze, which was fully extinguished just over an hour and a half later.

The damage to 44-6504 was assessed and ten days later the aircraft was transferred to the 2nd Strategic Air Depot at Little Staughton in Bedfordshire for repair, which necessitated a complete inner and outer wing panel change. The bomber was flown back to Molesworth on 8th November and returned to service on 20th November with a mission to Gelsenkirchen in north-west Germany. This was followed by participation in another eight missions before 44-6504 took off on what proved to be its final flight.

The Crash

At 08.15 hours on 16th December 1944 a force of B-17s from the 303rd Bomb Group began to take off from Molesworth on a mission to bomb the marshalling yards at Ulm in southern Germany. The weather report for the day was poor but the decision was given for the mission to go ahead as planned. All got away safely and headed for the assembly point far out over the North Sea; but at 10.15 hours, with the weather showing no signs of improvement, a message was relayed to abort the mission and for all bombs to be jettisoned over the North Sea. By now Molesworth was fog-bound, so the bombers began to scatter and head for the diversionary airfield of RAF Kirmington in Lincolnshire.

Thick cloud made it difficult for the crew of 44-6504 to jettison their bombs, as did the shipping they saw below every time they were able to see through the clouds, so the decision was made to return to base with the bombs still on board. Unfortunately the radio compass and GEE receiver (a medium-range radio aid to navigation and target identification) began to act in an erratic manner, leaving the navigator unable to get a fix on their position. The crew were now completely lost; but a third-class radio fix was obtained at 12.30 hours, followed shortly thereafter by a second-class fix which confirmed their position. At this point the pilot, 2nd Lieutenant Kyle, mistakenly thinking they were back on course, removed his seat belt and informed the rest of the crew that they were on their way home.

The fix, however, had put them some twenty miles north of Cheviot summit at an altitude of just under 2,000 feet, severe icing having been experienced above this height. The crew, not knowing the area, were oblivious to the fact that the high ground of the England/Scotland border lay just ahead and at 13.15 hours, whilst gaining altitude, the bomber struck the top of West Hill in blizzard conditions, narrowly missing a rocky outcrop known as Braydon Crag. The nose of the aircraft was completely crushed on impact, killing Sergeant Turner and Flying Officer Holcombe. Up in the cockpit, Kyle was seriously injured when one of the propellers smashed through the cockpit and broke his jaw.

As soon as the aircraft stopped moving, Flying Officer Hardy pulled open the emergency escape hatch and exited, whereupon he met Sergeant Schieferstein. Hardy then re-entered the bomber's fuselage and dragged out the seriously injured Kyle, who was bleeding heavily from his head wound. Thinking they were the only survivors of the crash, the three made their way downhill to the west, fortuitously arriving at Mount Hooly Farm in the valley below. As the three crossed a stream in the valley bottom, they were spotted by a shepherd who, thinking they were Germans, used his shotgun to fire a number of warning shots! Once they had identified themselves as Americans they were taken into the farm, where Kyle, being the more seriously injured, was laid down on some straw in a barn.

Meanwhile, in a valley to the north, two shepherds, John Dagg of Dunsdale and Frank Moscrop of Southernknowe, had heard the B-17 passing overhead. When the sound of the engines stopped, both surmised that the aircraft had crashed. Dagg, accompanied by his Border collie, Sheila, set off up the hillside, following the western edge of Bizzle Ravine. He was followed later by Moscrop and a third shepherd, Arch Bertram.

On reaching the summit, Dagg released Sheila so that she could help locate any survivors while he searched the area. Later, just after all three shepherds had met up, Sheila came running back very excited and barking. Dagg and Moscrop followed her as she led them to four airmen huddled together in a peat hag, trying to keep warm; these were Sergeants Berly, Delaney, Kaufmann and Smith. Delaney had a head wound, which the shepherds wrapped with some parachute silk. Berly had lost his flying boots whilst trying to put out a fire in the bomb bay, so some more of the silk was wrapped around his feet. Moscrop was informed that there had been a crew of nine aboard the B-17 and, despite being warned that there were bombs on board and that it would be dangerous to do so, he went to the wreckage to search for more survivors. Having found no one else in the wreckage, Moscrop returned to rejoin the others.

Slipping and sliding, the three shepherds led the four airmen down the hillside, and the group eventually arrived at Dunsdale Farm at about 18.30 hours. Soon, news reached them that three other crewmen had survived and were at Mount Hooly Farm; but just as this news was filtering through, the bombs within the wreckage of the B-17 exploded.

Despite knowing that the bombs had exploded on the mountain top, John Dagg returned to the crash site and with the aid of a hurricane lamp, searched in vain all night for the two crewmen who were still unaccounted for. The following day a team from RAF Milfield arrived to search the crash scene. Sadly, at 15.00 hours the bodies of Turner and Holcombe were located amidst the twisted wreckage.

All seven survivors were taken to a military hospital at RAF Milfield. Kyle, who was the most severely injured, was later taken by ambulance to Newcastle General Hospital where he spent 3½ months recovering from his injuries and an operation to help rebuild his face.

The Aftermath

John Dagg and Frank Moscrop were awarded the British Empire Medal for their part in the search for survivors. Sheila the Border collie received the Dicken Medal, the animal equivalent of the Victoria Cross, the only civilian dog to receive what is the highest award bestowed on animals. The awards were presented at a gathering of locals and RAF and USAAF representatives close to Dunsdale Farm in July 1945. A scroll was presented

Crashed 16th December 1944

B17 44-6504 on fire at base on 19th October 1944. (B. Hallum)

In 1945, a 'passing of the scrolls' ceremony was held in honour of the shepherds who helped rescue Allied airmen during the Second World War. (College Valley Estates)

to the Shepherds of The Cheviot thanking them for their help in the rescue of airmen from these hills.

With most accidents the story would end there, leaving it to be related down the years in books such as this. However, in 1967, interest in the story was rekindled when a local boys' club, The Reivers, made up of members of the St Michael's Boys Choir based in Alnwick, stumbled across the part-buried remains of the B-17 whilst walking The Cheviot. Following an extremely dry summer the peat around the boggy bomb craters, which since the crash had been an impenetrable swamp, had dried out and exposed the wreckage.

Whilst rummaging around amongst the wreckage, members of The Reivers stumbled across two micro-switches. Attached to each micro-switch was the manufacturer's data plate, the information thereon suggesting that they had been manufactured by Honeywell in Illinois, USA. The micro-switches were mailed to Honeywell who established that they formed part of the B-17's Norden bomb-sight. Tests carried out on the micro-switches revealed that one of them was still in working order. Keen to learn more about the find, Honeywell contacted the US Air Force and details of the crash and the rescue of the survivors by the shepherds and dog were established for the first time since the war.

Following further excavations at the crash site, The Reivers unearthed one of the Wright Cyclone engines and recovered a propeller blade from another. This recovered blade was used to form a memorial on Braydon Crag in honour of the two USAAF airmen who had died in the crash. The memorial was unveiled on 29th May 1968 in a ceremony attended by local residents and members of The Reivers. As the ceremony at Braydon Crag took place, surviving members of the crew and representatives of the US Air Force gathered in New York and initiated a transatlantic link using the still-working micro-switch recovered from the B-17. As the memorial was unveiled the Last Post was sounded, and at that moment a flight of four F-100 Super Sabre fighters from the 20th Tactical Fighter Wing carried out a flypast to honour those who had died in the crash. Sadly, in the mid-1980s the plaque and propeller were stolen from the crash site. No trace of them has ever been found despite numerous enquiries in the region.

Two of the surviving crew returned to the crash site in 1995, when a memorial was unveiled in the College Valley in memory of all those Allied airmen who lost their lives in the Cheviot Hills. The memorial was erected by Service personnel based at RAF Boulmer to commemorate the 50th anniversary of the end of the Second World War in Europe. George Kyle and Joel Berly, who had kept in touch since the war, attended the unveiling and were taken back to the crash site in an RAF Sea King helicopter from RAF Boulmer.

The event was covered by local TV news and watched by Jim Corbett from his home in Newcastle, unaware that the event had taken place. Jim had visited the crash site in the autumn of 1983, his dad having used the story as an incentive to get him walking the Cheviot Hills. Little did his dad know that a seemingly innocuous remark about the wreckage of an aircraft being on the walk would result in the two of them travelling the length and breadth of Great Britain in search of other aircraft wrecks; searches that would eventually result in the formation of the Air Crash Investigation and Archaeology group (ACIA) in 2001.

Jim always had an affinity with the B-17 crash, it being the first aircraft wreck he had ever found, and he longed to trace the pilot – if he was still alive. Watching the report on TV set in motion a series of events that culminated in Jim meeting George Kyle in June 2000, the intention being to guide George's daughter, Carol Kyle Sage, who had been unable to attend the unveiling of the memorial in 1995, to the crash site itself.

Jim and the Kyle family went on to become great friends and met twice more before Jim became the proud father of twins, Daniel and Sophie, in November 2004. Jim named his son Daniel Kyle Corbett in honour of his great friend, a gesture which left George Kyle overwhelmed with emotion when he was told over the telephone not long after the twins' birth.

Sadly, George Kyle was never to meet his namesake; he passed away peacefully in a Fort Lauderdale hospital less than a year later on 20th September 2005. A few months before his death, George arranged a meeting with his partner, Kitty van Sickler, and daughter Carol at his apartment in Fort Lauderdale, Florida. He explained that when his time came he would like to be cremated, which to Kitty and Carol seemed a reasonable request. But his next request took them by surprise: he stated that he wanted his ashes to be returned to Great Britain and scattered at the crash site of his B-17.

On 4th October 2006, the family returned to Great Britain to carry out

George's final wish. With them travelled Jay Hardy, the son of co-pilot James Hardy, and his wife Jeri. A helicopter was arranged to take Jim Corbett, Carol, Kitty, Jay and Jeri to the crash site for what was a very emotional experience for all of them.

In April 2008 a room forming part of a Youth Hostel Association bunkhouse at Mount Hooly Farm at the foot of the mountain, was named in honour of George Kyle. Unveiled by Lord Joicey on 10th April, the room, which includes stories and photos relating to the crash, was named the Kyle Room in his memory; a fitting and permanent tribute to a truly remarkable man and dear friend, who is sadly missed.

The Crash Site

Large sections of the B-17 can still be found scattered over a wide area to the south-east of Braydon Crag. The main undercarriage legs are nearly 500 yards apart, blown away from the main site when the bombs exploded. Other parts can be found further away, dragged from the crash site over the years by souvenir hunters. Some 60 yards north-west of the main bomb crater are signs of the first impact, with three gouges formed by the inboard engines and fuselage still being evident. A survey of this area by ACIA members in 2006 revealed remnants of the ball turret, which was ripped off when the aircraft struck the mountain.

Many of the intact sections, including two of the engines and the tail gunner's position, have been removed to museums, one of the engines being on display at the Bamburgh Castle Aviation Museum. The tail gunner's position was with the North East Aircraft Museum but is now outside the region.

Visitors to this crash site are reminded that the ashes of George Kyle are scattered here. We would appreciate it if you would treat the site with the respect it rightly deserves.

Jim Corbett

6

Bristol Beaufighter IIF T3037

Aircraft Type:	Bristol Beaufighter IIF
Serial:	T3037
Code(s):	NOT KNOWN
Unit:	No 406 (Lynx) Squadron, RCAF
Base:	RAF Acklington, Northumberland
Crew:	Pilot: Pilot Officer Herbert B. Wooler Radar Operator/Observer: Sergeant Trevor Williams
Crash Date:	8th January 1942
Crash Location:	Widdrington, Northumberland
Grid Reference:	81/237944

The Aircraft

In 1938, as the threat of war in Europe grew, the RAF was desperately short of day-fighters with the performance necessary to enable them to intercept and down the new generation of German twin-engined bombers. Aware of this shortage and the problems affecting development of one proposed solution, the Westland Whirlwind single-seat twin-engined fighter, the Bristol Aeroplane Company put forward a proposal to develop a fighter version of its twin-engined Beaufort torpedo bomber (see Chapter 7) as an interim solution to fill the fighter gap. The Air Ministry duly granted Bristol permission to take a part-built Beaufort I off the production line and use it as the basis for what became the Beaufighter.

The new aircraft combined the Beaufort's wings, tail unit and landing gear with a shortened, fighter-style forward fuselage and a pair of Bristol Hercules radial engines that offered significantly more power than the Beaufort's Taurus power plants. The two-man crew comprised the pilot and his observer, the latter being positioned aft of the pilot and beneath a Perspex blister which had replaced the Beaufort's dorsal turret. The result was a robust and stable gun platform which, though designed as a stop-gap, went on to prove its versatility as, amongst other things, a night-fighter, torpedo bomber, and anti-shipping strike aircraft.

Impressed by what they saw, the Air Ministry issued Specification F17/39 and rewarded Bristol's private-venture proposal with an order for four prototypes (R2052–5) and an initial batch of 300 production aircraft. The first prototype flew on 17th July 1939 fitted with Hercules I-SM engines. Over the following weeks R2053–5 were flight-tested with Hercules I-M, III and II engines, with varying degrees of success.

The first production model, the Beaufighter IF (F for Fighter), entered service with the Fighter Interception Unit at RAF Tangmere in West Sussex on 12th August 1940 and conducted the type's first operation on the night of 4th/5th September. By late October the Mk IF had entered service with RAF Fighter Command's No 29 Squadron at RAF Debden in Essex, followed by Nos 25, 219 (Mysore), 600 (City of London) and 604 (County of Middlesex) Squadrons. All of these units operated the Mk IF in the night-fighter role, with AI (Airborne Interception) Mk IV radar equipment housed in the fuselage. The combination of the AI Mk IV and ferocious firepower (four nose-mounted 20mm cannons, four .303 calibre machine guns in the starboard wing and two .303s in the port wing) proved extremely potent.

The Beaufighter IF's first night 'kill' – achieved without the aid of AI – was scored by No 604 Squadron on 19th November 1940, when Flight Lieutenant John 'Cat's Eyes' Cunningham downed a Ju 88 bomber. It was also during this period that Guy Gibson (who later won the VC leading the famous Dams raid) flew some 99 night-fighter sorties with No 29 Squadron, shooting down three enemy aircraft and winning a Bar to his DFC.

The Beaufighter IF was also used as a long-range day-fighter over the Mediterranean and Western Desert, after some 80 examples were fitted with desert equipment and had their range extended thanks to auxiliary fuel tanks in the fuselage (later replaced by extra fuel tanks in the outer wing-panels, but at the expense of the wing-mounted machine guns). The long-range day-fighter role was also the domain of the Beaufighter IC (C for Coastal; fitted with additional radio and navigation equipment), which began to replace the Blenheim IVF in RAF Coastal Command in December

Crashed 8th January 1942

A Bristol Beaufighter Mk II in flight. Like T3037, which crashed at Widdington in 1942, this aircraft (R2270) also served with 406 Squadron at Acklington. **(J. Shipley)**

1940. In all, 914 Beaufighter IFs and ICs were built before production switched to the Mk II.

Despite the Beaufighter's early successes, construction and delivery of the Short Stirling four-engined bomber, which also made use of the Bristol Hercules power plant, was deemed more important. Thus Hercules production was directed to supply the Stirling production line, which in turn raised fears of a shortage of supply for the three Beaufighter lines. To counter this, the next major production model, the Beaufighter IIF, was fitted with two Rolls-Royce Merlin XX inline engines.

RAF Fighter Command used the Mk IIF as a home-defence night-fighter; other examples equipped Fleet Air Arm units. The new power plant adversely affected the Beaufighter's longitudinal stability, but this was remedied to an extent by fitting a new tailplane with twelve degrees of dihedral. The addition of a dorsal fin extension helped to cure a tendency to swing on take-off.

Unfortunately the Merlin XX-powered Mk IIFs also suffered from engine reliability problems and had disappointing performance compared to Hercules-powered Beaufighters; and production ceased after 450 examples. Front-line squadrons equipped with Mk IIFs soon relinquished them, and many subsequently found their way to training units.

The Crash

At 21.05 hours on 8th January 1942, Beaufighter II T3037 took off from RAF Acklington on a night Ground Controlled Interception (GCI) exercise. At the controls was Pilot Officer Herbert Wooler, with Sergeant Trevor Williams acting as his radar operator. Originally from St Andrew in Jamaica, Wooler, aged 22, had enlisted on 2nd September 1940. After initial pilot training (and becoming a Pilot Officer on 16th August 1941), he undertook a final spell of training with No 54 OTU, then was posted to No 406 (Lynx) Squadron, Royal Canadian Air Force (RCAF), which he joined on 28th November 1941. He had a total flying time of 176 hours of which 27 were on Beaufighters (nine of them at night). Williams, aged 21, was from Llandilo in South Wales; it was his duty to operate the radar equipment, and thus direct his pilot into the 'kill'.

No 406 Squadron was formed at RAF Acklington in Northumberland on 16th May 1941, and was the first Canadian night-fighter squadron. Initially equipped with Bristol Blenheims, it soon converted to Beaufighters, and during the night of 1st/2nd September 1941, though still not fully operational, claimed its first victory when Flying Officer Fumerton and Sergeant Bing shot down a Ju 88A-4 (see Chapter 17). This was the first confirmed 'kill' both for the squadron and for a Canadian night-fighter unit. By the end of 1941 the squadron had scored another five confirmed night-time 'kills'.

Exactly what happened during the final short flight of Beaufighter IIF T3037 is unclear. The take-off was uneventful, but just ten minutes later the aircraft was seen emerging from cloud, and apparently stalling before going into a spin. Pilot Officer Wooler never regained control and just after 21.15 hours the aircraft crashed on the edge of a small wood at Stobswood Colliery, near Widdrington Station (barely missing two houses). Both Pilot Officer Wooler and Sergeant Williams died on impact.

At the time of the crash Mrs Defty was living in Woodburn House, and her parents lived in Alma House across the garden. Both houses were (and still are) bordered to the west by a small wood which Mrs Defty's father used to cut through to get to his workplace at the brickworks. On the night of the crash, her parents were in Alma House with her sister who had just given birth, and were in the upstairs corner room of the house, while Mrs Defty was in her own house with her youngest child, when they heard a terrible loud noise outside. Nothing could prepare them for what they were to see as they looked outside for the source of the noise.

In the gardens between the houses, wreckage from an aircraft lay scattered everywhere, while trees and a large section of hedge had been completely ripped up. Mrs Defty's husband, who was an Air Raid Precautions warden, went out immediately and found the remains of the two dead airmen, both of whom had been thrown clear of the cockpit when it broke up after colliding with trees prior to hitting the ground. It was already clear how lucky Mrs Defty and her family had been, with wreckage completely blocking the garden, and one of the wings propped up against her parents' wall.

It did not take long for the emergency services to arrive, along with a team from RAF Acklington, only a short distance away. The two bodies were recovered and laid out in the ambulance shed at the bottom of the drive to Woodburn House. Throughout the night various officials visited the site, before the 'experts' arrived the following day to investigate the crash. The investigation was followed by a clean-up period during which time the family were not allowed to leave by the front of the house – much to the annoyance of Mrs Defty's father, who could no longer take his usual short cut to work!

The Aftermath

The result of the investigation seemed to suggest that instrument failure was the cause of the accident, with the Form 1180 (Loss Card) stating that the aircraft lost control in the clouds and went into a spin whilst flying on instruments. It goes on to say that it is 'not possible to determine whether the accident was caused by faulty instrument flying or an instrument failure owing to the extensive damage of the a/c'. What does seem certain is that, after going into a dive, the aircraft hit trees on the edge of the wood just before the houses, which dissipated the energy of the fall and probably saved both properties – but especially Alma House – from destruction.

T3037 had only been with No 406 Squadron since 28th December 1941 after arriving from No 19 Maintenance Unit, to which it had been delivered on 9th October; thus the aircraft's life was cut short along with the lives of Wooler and Williams.

At 14.30 hours on 13th January 1942 the body of Herbert Wooler was laid to rest in Chevington Cemetery, just a short distance from the crash site. Six of his fellow pilot officers on No 406 Squadron acted as pallbearers; six airmen of 'B' Flight provided a guard of honour. Also in attendance was Mr S. S. Wooler, Herbert's uncle, and Mr Shaw, a family friend. Meanwhile, a few hundred miles away, the body of Sergeant Trevor Williams was laid to rest in the churchyard of the Calvinistic Methodist Chapel in his native Llandilo.

The Crash Site

The quiet gardens of Woodburn House and Alma House show no signs of what happened on that night in January 1942. The hedge that divides the two properties, which was damaged by the aircraft, has since grown back, and it would seem that the majority of the wreckage lay on the surface.

Jonathan Shipley

The crash site as it appears today from the garden of Woodburn House, looking towards Alma House. The aircraft had hit the trees to the right, breaking up and scattering wreckage across the garden. Most of the hedge was destroyed, with some wreckage coming to rest against Alma House. (J. Shipley)

Bristol Beaufort I L9797

Aircraft Type:	Bristol Beaufort I
Serial:	L9797
Code(s):	OA–F
Unit:	No 22 Squadron, RAF
Base:	RAF North Coates, Lincolnshire
Crew:	Pilot: Pilot Officer Richard D. Westlake Observer: Sergeant Sydney G. Twitchen Wireless Operator: Sergeant Llewellyn E. T. Harris Air Gunner: Sergeant Patrick O'Flaherty
Civilian fatalities	Henry Cox Eleanor Cox Gladys Cox
Crash Date:	6th June 1940
Crash Location:	77 Fifth Row, Ashington, Northumberland
Grid Reference:	81/259878

The Aircraft

The Bristol Beaufort was designed to meet Air Ministry Specification M15/35 (torpedo bomber) and Specification G24/35 (general reconnaissance/light bomber), both of which reflected an urgent need to re-equip and modernise RAF Coastal Command's front-line squadrons in the late 1930s. The general reconnaissance/light bomber requirement was met by another Bristol design, the three-seat Blenheim IV, an adaptation of which formed the basis of the company's submission to meet the torpedo bomber requirement.

The Air Ministry, however, stipulated that the new torpedo bomber had

A Bristol Beaufort I.

to have a crew of four to better meet operational requirements. Bristol's response, the Beaufort, was a scaled-up version of the Blenheim IV with redesigned accommodation (hence the distinctive high roof-line back to the dorsal turret) and a slightly lengthened fuselage to enable carriage of a torpedo in a semi-exposed position. Power was to come from two Bristol Perseus radial engines, but it soon became clear that these could not provide sufficient power for a four-man torpedo bomber whose gross weight had increased by some 25 per cent.

An order for 78 Beaufort Is was placed in August 1936, but first flight of the prototype (L4441) was delayed until 15th October 1938, in part because of overheating problems with the more powerful Bristol Taurus II engine, which had been selected to replace the Perseus. Competing against the Beaufort was the Blackburn Botha I (see Chapter 3), the initial promise of which failed to materialise once it took to the air powered by Perseus engines. The Beaufort, too, had its share of teething problems, but it was easily the more capable of the two designs. Consequently, because Taurus engines were in short supply, they were assigned to the Beaufort, leaving the Botha to make do with the disappointing Perseus.

The Beaufort I, production of which totalled 1,013, entered RAF service with No 22 Squadron at RAF Thorney Island in Hampshire in November 1939; the first of six Coastal Command squadrons to re-equip with the type. The offensive payload consisted of one semi-recessed torpedo or up to 1,500 pounds of bombs or mines. Defensive armament in early aircraft comprised .303 calibre machine guns in the nose (one or two), dorsal turret (two) and wings (one in each). Later aircraft had an extra .303 in a blister below the nose and one in each beam position.

It wasn't until the night of 15th/16th April 1940 that the Beaufort – the RAF's principal torpedo bomber from 1940–3 – made its operational debut when No 22 Squadron, which by then had moved to RAF North Coates in Lincolnshire, carried out a mine-laying operation (Coastal Command's first of the war) in the mouth of the River Jade. The operation marked the beginning of the Beaufort's extensive anti-shipping operations in home waters and enemy coastal waters alike, including attacks on the German battle-cruisers *Scharnhorst*, *Gneisenau* and *Prinz Eugen*. RAF Beaufort Is also operated further afield, flying from bases in Malta and the Western Desert.

Part of the second production batch of 137 aircraft, Beaufort I L9797 was fitted with Taurus II engines (126803 and 126820) and was taken on charge at No 6 Maintenance Unit at RAF Brize Norton in Oxfordshire on 7th March 1940. On 30th March 1940 it was delivered to No 22 Squadron.

The Crash

At 21.45 hours on 5th June 1940, with darkness setting in, L9797 and seven other Bristol Beaufort Is from No 22 Squadron took off from RAF North Coates in Lincolnshire and headed out across the North Sea on an operation to attack oil dumps and refineries at Ghent in Belgium (although some sources have suggested that the Flushing area of the Netherlands was actually the target). One aircraft was forced to return early due to a loss of oil pressure in an engine.

The pilot of L9797 on this operation was Pilot Officer Richard Westlake, a pre-war member of the RAF who had been granted his wings on 22nd May 1937 after training at No 11 Flight Training School at RAF Wittering in Cambridgeshire. He was granted the rank of Pilot Officer on 1st April 1940. Flying with him were Sergeant Twitchen (aged 22), Sergeant Harris (20) and Sergeant O'Flaherty (23), all of whom appear to have joined No 22 Squadron during late April and early May 1940. During this period the RAF

***Jim Slaughter (right) alongside his brother Ernie (left), and neighbour Freddy Weddell (centre) in the garden of their house on Long Row. Jim and Eric were in the house when Beaufort L9797 crashed into the street behind.* (J. Slaughter)**

carried out a number of raids against coastal targets in support of the troop withdrawal after the fall of France, and against the invasion fleet that the Germans were starting to build for the invasion of Great Britain.

It is not clear what happened to L9797 during the operation, but it can be assumed that the aircraft reached the target as it had no bombs on board when, at about 01.30 hours on 6th June, the residents of Ashington in Northumberland heard the sound of aero engines low overhead. The air raid siren had sounded a few hours earlier, so a state of alert was still in force when L9797 stared to circle.

Jim Slaughter, an Ashington lad who lived in Long Row (adjacent to where L9797 crashed), remembers the night well. His father had returned from night shift at the colliery and had been pacing back and forth from the house's front-room window to its rear window, watching the aircraft circle overhead. His mother heard him walking around and had just moved to the front-room window, beside Jim and his three brothers, when she saw a black shape looming out of the night sky. By the time she let out a scream, the boys were at the rear window, and the house at the end of the garden behind was in flames.

Jim's father had watched the final seconds of the Beaufort's flight as it came over the roof of their house; the starboard wing clipped the garden before the hulk of the plane went into 77 Fifth Row. One engine tore straight through the house, demolished out-buildings to the rear and continued across the road, hitting colliery wagons behind. Downstairs, the mother and father of the household, Henry Cox, aged 52, and Eleanor Cox, aged 48, were killed instantly. As the fire spread their daughter, Gladys Cox, aged 18, jumped from the window in flames, and was taken to a house on Fourth Row before being moved to Ashington Hospital where she later died. Still in the house was the youngest son, William, who was not rescued for some time.

By now many people from the Colliery Rows had gathered, and noticed two parachutes falling to earth. With the invasion panic at its height, people were unsure if the two airmen drifting down from the sky were British or German, so they immediately made for them. Realising that they might be mistaken for the enemy, the two men – Pilot Officer Westlake and Sergeant Twitchen – shouted as they drifted down that they were English. Westlake landed in a tree a short distance to the north-west of where L9797 had crashed, while Twitchen landed in a tree in the front garden of Long Row.

With the fire now in full blaze, Westlake and Twitchen were asked if there were any bombs on board their aircraft, to which they replied no, but that there was a lot of ammunition. This duly started going off in the inferno as locals manned stirrup-pumps alongside the Fire Service in an attempt to quell the flames. When William Cox was finally recovered from the wreckage of his home, he was taken to hospital where he remained for several months while his burns were treated.

The Aftermath

So what caused Beaufort I L9797 to crash? The Form 1180 (Loss Card) for the incident records that the aircraft had bombed oil dumps and refineries at Ghent. Whilst approaching the English coast on the return to base, the pilot was dazzled by searchlights and became lost amongst barrage balloons. He opened up the engines, but the aircraft started to vibrate and the cockpit filled with fumes. The pilot then put the aircraft on a course out to sea, and gave the order for the crew to bail out. However, the report goes on to say that, after gliding some distance, the aircraft suddenly turned around and went into a dive, then crashed into a row of houses. It confirms that both the wireless operator and air gunner were killed, but that on recovery of the bodies, one was found to be wearing his parachute, it having become entangled with the aircraft (presumably during the process of bailing out) and thus dragged him down with it. The parachute of the other crewman was found some distance away without its ripcord.

The crash totally destroyed 77 Fifth Row, and damaged the two houses on either side. The fact that the Beaufort tipped slightly in its final seconds, allowing the starboard wing to hit the gardens just before impact, so that the aircraft scythed into the street at an angle, no doubt saved those houses and their occupants from the same fate as that of the Cox family.

In the weeks that followed the crash the site was cleared, although Jim Slaughter recalled seeing a large section of wing, complete with RAF roundel, propped up against a house next door for some time afterwards; and people collecting Perspex from which they made trinkets. Mrs Isabel Stephen (*née* King) of Ashington also recalled many local children visiting the site over the following days and weeks, but that her parents would not let her visit due to the dreadful loss of life.

The three members of the Cox family were buried together in the churchyard of Holy Sepulchre Church in Ashington, just a short distance from the house in which they died. Jim Slaughter recalled the bodies of the two airmen who died being recovered and laid out on colliery doors, before being removed by the RAF. Sergeant Patrick O'Flaherty, a native of Kiltimagh, County Mayo, was laid to rest a short distance up the coast

The grave of Sergeant O'Flaherty, the air gunner on L9797, in Chevington Cemetery. **(J. Shipley)**

at Chevington Cemetery, where he lies with many other airmen who died over Northumberland. Sergeant Llewellyn Harris was interred in Portsmouth Kingston Cemetery.

William Cox spent a long time recovering from the injuries he sustained as a result of the crash, and his cousin recalled how William had problems with his right arm for the rest of his life. Many other locals remember him working as a barman at the Grand Hotel in Ashington in later years.

It is not clear what happened to Pilot Officer Westlake after the crash, although it is known that he continued in the RAF and became a Flying Officer on 1st April 1941, then a Flight Lieutenant on 1st April 1942.

Sergeant Sydney Twitchen was not so lucky, being killed a matter of months after the crash of L9797 whilst on operations with No 22 Squadron. He was the Observer in Beaufort N1146/OA–R when it took off from RAF Bircham Newton in Norfolk at 01.30 hours on 10th September 1940 on a mission to attack targets in Boulogne. The last contact from the Beaufort was a wireless transmission at 02.40 hours, and it is assumed the aircraft went down in the North Sea. The body of the pilot, Sergeant R. D. Gunn, was washed up on a Norfolk beach, and is buried at Old Catton in Norfolk; that of the air gunner, Sergeant C. S. F. Beer, was washed up on Texel (one of the Frisian Islands) on 28th September 1940.

The bodies of Sergeant Twitchen and the wireless operator, Sergeant J. Murray, were never recovered and so their names are inscribed on the Runnymede Memorial in Surrey, which commemorates all those who lost their lives during the Second World War whilst serving with the air forces of the Commonwealth at bases in Great Britain or in North-western Europe, and who have no known grave.

The Crash Site

There are no reminders of the tragic events of June 1940 at the crash site today. Locals do not remember 77 Fifth Row ever being rebuilt, although they do recall wreckage remaining on site for some weeks after the event. In the years that followed, many of the colliery houses were pulled down to make way for new developments. The site where Beaufort L9797 came to grief is now under a housing estate, with a garage and shops occupying the land where coal trucks once stood.

Jonathan Shipley

8

De Havilland DH89A Dragon Rapide G-AFMF

Aircraft Type:	**De Havilland DH89A Dragon Rapide**
Registration:	G-AFMF
Operator:	Oldstead Airways
Base:	Newcastle Airport
Pilot:	Brian K. Waugh
Passengers:	Walter Glover John Harper Dennis Jolly Robin Phillips Monty Rosen Harvey Shenker Allan Smith
Crash Date:	19th February 1954
Crash Location:	Simonburn Common, Simonburn, Northumberland
Grid Reference:	87/836730

The Aircraft

The de Havilland DH89 Dragon Rapide light transport was designed in 1933 as a successor to the DH84 Dragon, which had a short production run of only 115 aircraft. The prototype DH89, known as the Dragon Six, first flew on 17th April 1934 powered by two de Havilland Gypsy Six inline piston engines. Production Dragon Rapides, 731 of which were built, were faster and more comfortable than the DH84 Dragon, and proved popular with short-haul operators in the pre-war years. The DH89A Dragon Rapide featured small trailing-edge flaps on the lower set of wings, these being introduced on aircraft built from 1937 onwards. Some 200 Dragon Rapides

Crashed 19th February 1954

A de Havilland Dragon Rapide G-AFMF. **(R. Waugh)**

had been delivered to civil operators around the world by the time war broke out in September 1939.

Oldstead Airways' G-AFMF was a DH89A variant built at de Havilland's famous Hatfield factory in Hertfordshire in 1938. It was purchased new by Airwork Ltd based at Heston Aerodrome in Middlesex on 9th December 1938 and was issued with its Certificate of Airworthiness on 20th January 1939. From the moment it was purchased G-AFMF was on the move. It went first to the Martin School of Air Navigation at Shoreham Airport in West Sussex; then on to No 7 Civil Air Navigation School at Perth on Tayside, followed by transfers to No 7 Air Observation Navigation School (AONS) on 30th January 1939 and No 6 AONS on 23rd May 1940 (both also based at Perth), all of these being units of the RAF.

On 15th July 1940 G-AFMF was impressed into RAF service as a Dominie II (the name adopted for militarised Dragon Rapides) and given the serial Z7256, its silver dope paint being painted over with green and brown camouflage. During its RAF service Z7256 operated in a communications role, carrying wireless operators at the very beginning of their training as they undertook their first air navigation exercises. The aircraft survived the Second World War pretty much unscathed, though a minor accident on 8th March 1942 resulted in it having to be taken out of service for two months, most of which was spent in storage.

By the time the aircraft was purchased by its final owner, John Weston Adamson, trading as Oldstead Airways, on 18th April 1950, it had already served with no fewer than eleven operators.

The Crash

A scramble of press and photographers surrounded G-AFMF at Newcastle Airport on the morning of 19th February 1954, eager to record the departure of seven young boxing hopefuls from Durham University who were about to set off for Dublin to take part in universities and hospitals championships.

At the scene of the crash.
(Pauline Nicholson)

Crashed 19th February 1954

Flying the Dragon Rapide that morning was Brian Waugh, an employee of Oldstead Airways, a small charter company based at the airport since it had formed in 1950. Brian had served as an air gunner during World War II but longed to fly as pilot, and his dream came true in October 1950 when he was issued with his Private Pilot's Licence.

The aircraft took off at 08.50 hours and almost immediately entered a thick overcast. Conditions worsened as the flight headed west, and as the aircraft climbed through 3,000 feet Brian Waugh noticed ice forming on the windscreen and the airspeed indicator began to fluctuate. Having opened the side window panel, Waugh peered out and saw a thick layer of ice on the wing leading-edges and interplane bracing struts. Almost immediately the aircraft began to vibrate and refused to climb above 3,000 feet. Realising that the flight controls had become very sluggish, Waugh decided to abandon the flight and turned onto a reciprocal heading. A minute or so later the aircraft dived uncontrollably towards the ground.

Struggling with the controls, Waugh had just managed to pull the aircraft level when it struck the ground heavily, bounced, then impacted with soft moorland and immediately caught fire. John Harper, who was sitting in the front passenger seat on the port side, was partly flung out of the aircraft and found himself lying on his back on the ground when flames burst from one of the engines over his right shoulder. Unable to move, Harper shouted and someone who was lying across his legs moved, allowing Harper to get up and run clear.

Harper was standing about 40 yards from the burning wreck when Robin Philips and Dennis Jolly approached, dragging the seriously injured Brian Waugh with them. A shout from within the burning aircraft alerted Harper who ran to the aid of the trapped passenger. As he approached the aircraft he came across Monty Rosen who was trying to pull Walter Glover from the wreckage. Together they managed to pull Glover, who was still trapped in his seat, from inside the burning Dragon.

Two more passengers, Allan Smith and Harvey Shenker, had managed to escape through the broken nose of the aircraft. Eventually all of them were free and they gathered around the injured pilot, who had suffered two broken ankles.

Visibility was almost nil and, after some time, when it became clear that nobody was coming to their aid, it was decided that Rosen and Harper, the two uninjured passengers, should set off for help. Brian used his wartime RAF survival training and advised them that, if they found a stream, they were to follow it as it would almost certainly lead them to habitation. The pair set off and eventually reached the farm of Burn House about two miles from the crash site; from there they were directed down the road to Simonburn where they raised the alarm.

Unknown to Rosen and Harper, Brian Waugh also instructed another pair of the passengers to head off in a different direction and by following another stream, they arrived at Tecket Farm at almost the same time as Rosen and Harper reached Simonburn.

Emergency services from Hexham were soon at the crash site, accessing the moor from the nearby farm of Stooprigg, only half a mile from where G-AFMF came down and clearly visible from the crash site on a clear day, but totally obscured for the survivors that morning by the dense fog. They were all transferred by ambulance to Hexham Hospital and then the more seriously injured were transferred to a hospital in Newcastle. Thankfully, due to Brian Waugh's flying skills, all eight of them, including Waugh himself, made a full recovery.

The Aftermath

The post-crash investigation centred on whether the flight should have gone ahead at all. Brian Waugh argued that an error in a weather report, suggesting a freezing level of 15,000 feet instead of 1,500 feet, was to blame. But the investigating officer countered this by suggesting that a pilot with a Commercial Pilot's Licence should have sufficient knowledge of meteorology to realise that in mid-February, with a forecast of snow and sleet on high ground, a freezing level of 15,000 feet was most improbable.

Oldstead Airways were heavily fined for the crash. The costs involved proved too much for the small charter company and it folded. Brian Waugh went on to become one of the leading pioneers of aviation in New Zealand following his emigration to that country, helping to set up South Island Airways before retiring in 1967. Sadly, Brian died in 1984 following a heart attack; his funeral was a huge event – a fine send-off for someone who had played a significant part in New Zealand's early commercial aviation history.

Crashed 19th February 1954

The Crash Site

Examining some of the wreckage. **(A. Hudson)**

A surprisingly large amount of Dragon Rapide G–AFMF still exists at the crash site; among the more identifiable parts are one of the Gypsy Six engines, a metal propeller blade and crankshaft and two sections of flattened fuel tank. After the crash, no efforts were made by the authorities to recover the wreckage, it being left to the farmer on whose land the aircraft came down to dispose of it. He did this simply by digging a huge hole on the moor and burying the remainder of the aircraft on-site. The hole is still evident, as is the bare patch of ground where the aircraft burnt out, which is littered with tiny fragments of charred wood.

For many years the wreckage at this crash site had been incorrectly identified as a Tiger Moth reported as having crashed near Falstone on 1st March 1943. This was based solely on identification of the surviving Gypsy Six engine. However, closer examination of the wreckage in 2004 revealed a date of 1950 stamped on the crankshaft, which ties in with the purchase of G-AFMF by John Weston Adamson and its subsequent refit that same year before it entered service with Oldstead Airways.

In 2004 I had the pleasure of meeting Brian Waugh's son, the Reverend Richard Waugh, who was stopping off in Great Britain on return from the USA. This was Richard's first-ever visit to these shores and he was keen to visit the scene of his father's 1954 air crash. After visiting the site we drove to Newcastle Aero Club at Newcastle Airport, which in 1954 served as the terminal from which G-AFMF took off on its last flight.

Jim Corbett

9

De Havilland Venom FB4 WR557

Aircraft Type:	De Havilland Venom FB4
Serial:	WR557
Code(s):	NOT KNOWN
Unit:	No 22 Maintenance Unit, RAF
Base:	RAF Silloth, Cumbria
Crew:	Pilot: Flight Lieutenant W. F. Marshall
Crash Date:	4th March 1957
Crash Location:	Farlam Currick, Cumbria
Grid Reference:	86/640472

The Aircraft

The De Havilland Venom, known initially as the Vampire FB8, was outwardly very similar in appearance to its family predecessor, but in fact incorporated extensive redesign and marked a considerable advance in performance. The prototype Venom (VV612), which first flew at de Havilland's Hatfield plant in Hertfordshire on 2nd September 1949, retained the Vampire's characteristic fuselage pod and twin-boom configuration (originally adopted to keep the length of the jet tailpipe short and thus reduce loss of thrust); but the engine itself was changed from the de Havilland Goblin turbojet to the more powerful de Havilland Ghost.

The Ghost was a first-generation turbojet and as a result of the increase in performance that it offered, the Venom airframe was significantly improved. This included thinner wings with greater sweepback on the leading-edge; and repositioning of the long-range auxiliary fuel tanks from beneath the wings to the wing-tips. Improved aerodynamics led to greater speed – always of great benefit to a fighter.

Successful flight-testing led to an initial order for 370 Venom FB1s, and No 11 Squadron at Wunstorf in Germany became the first front-line squadron to fully re-equip with the type, in August 1952. The Venom FB1, which was armed with four 20mm cannons in the nose and up to 2,000 pounds of bombs or rocket-projectiles on underwing hardpoints, went on to form the backbone of 2nd Allied Tactical Air Force in Germany and also served in the RAF's Middle East Air Force.

***An example of a Venom* (Graham Nicholls)**

As with the Vampire, a two-seat night-fighter version of the Venom was developed. Known as the Venom NF2, it featured a wider fuselage for the pilot and radar operator (seated side by side) and an extended nose to house the radar. Just as the Venom FB1 had replaced Vampires in squadron service, so the Venom NF2 replaced the Vampire NF10 in RAF Fighter Command service from November 1953. A clear-view canopy was introduced on the Venom NF2A, which was followed by the Venom NF3 with power-operated ailerons, tail modifications, better radar and a more powerful engine.

Power-operated ailerons and redesigned tail surfaces featured on the next single-seat fighter-bomber variant, the Venom FB4, which also became the first member of the Venom family to be fitted with an ejector seat. The prototype Venom FB4 (WE381) first flew on 29th December 1953 and was followed by 150 production examples, the first of which entered service with No 6 Squadron at RAF Habbaniyah in Iraq in June 1955. The last Venom FB4s in RAF service were retired in July 1962.

The Crash

At 16.03 hours on 4th March 1957, Flight Lieutenant W. F. Marshall (Service No 166747), aged 31, took off from RAF Silloth in Cumbria in Venom FB4 WR557. Born in Newcastle, he had an 'above average' assessment which included a 'jet green' instrument rating; simply an assessment of a pilot's proficiency at instrument flying and his ability to land in bad weather. He was clearly a highly experienced pilot, having accumulated 2,494 flying hours which included 54 hours on the Venom. Furthermore, there was no indication that he had been involved in any previous accidents whilst serving at RAF Silloth, being well acquainted with all the correct emergency drills.

At 16.16 hours, just thirteen minutes after take-off, Marshall reported that he was experiencing difficulties; according to the RT Log he stated 'my elevator ... is jammed, returning to base, request homing and let-down'. His position at the time of this transmission was plotted by RAF Silloth and found to be 3½ miles north-north-east of Durham.

At 16.22 hours Flight Lieutenant Marshall again reported to RAF Silloth, this time informing them that he was at an altitude of 28,000 feet and that he intended to descend to 10,000 feet in order to burn fuel. No mention was made about jammed elevators. RAF Silloth felt there was no undue cause for concern and so advised a course of 290 degrees, cloud cover at base being 8/8 at 3,500 feet with 2⅓ miles' visibility. Caution was advised and Marshall was told to maintain a safety height of 4,800 feet and given a heading of 285 degrees to steer. These instructions were confirmed by Marshall at 16.25 hours, when he further advised RAF Silloth of his intention to descend from 10,000 feet to land back at the base.

Nothing more was ever heard from Flight Lieutenant Marshall, the crash of his Venom FB4 being estimated to have occurred at 16.27 hours. A 72-hour air, land and sea search was conducted for the stricken aircraft; but it was not until the afternoon of 7th March that a mountain rescue team spotted the wreckage scattered over more than 600 yards at a remote site some three to four miles from the nearest road. It was clear that the Venom had completely disintegrated on impact and it can only be presumed that Flight Lieutenant Marshall was killed instantly.

A helicopter was immediately despatched from RNAS Anthorn in Cumbria to recover the body of the pilot. As so often happens in these areas a thick mist quickly descended, grounding the helicopter after it had successfully landed next to the crash site. Visibility fell to just 25 yards, and it was feared that the helicopter and its crew would have to spend the night there. In the event, however, the mist dispersed as quickly as it had fallen and the helicopter departed for RAF Silloth with Flight Lieutenant Marshall's body. An armed guard was left at the crash site to prevent anyone tampering with the evidence.

Holding up a wing of the crashed Venom, clearly showing it was WR557.
(R. Gray)

The Aftermath

A search was conducted over four counties for evidence that could indicate why the accident had occurred, but nothing was found. The indications were that the aircraft was in no difficulties and that it flew into high ground at a normal angle of descent of five to ten degrees on a heading of 255 degrees. There were no signs of any use of flaps, the undercarriage had not been lowered and the pilot did not appear to have made any attempt to eject. In fact, there was no indication of the aircraft being stricken in any way.

The salvage unit, working under difficult conditions due to the remoteness of the crash site, removed the Venom's elevators to RAF Silloth, where they were carefully examined and found to be in full working order with full and free movement. No evidence was found that any part of the Venom had broken loose and damaged any of the control surfaces. So what could have happened?

It was concluded that Flight Lieutenant Marshall simply misread his instruments. But how could this have happened to an experienced pilot? Unfortunately at that time the altimeters used in many of the 'modern' jet

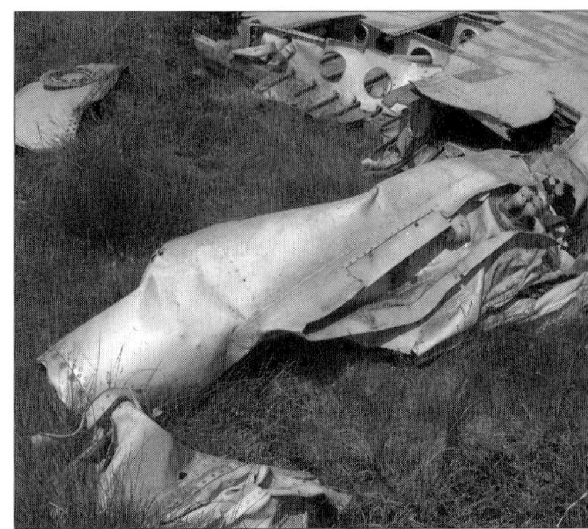

Engine parts (left) and the outer wing tank still remain at the site. (R. Gray)

fighters displayed the tens of thousands using a third pointer, rather than an odometer as in modern aircraft and cars. Furthermore, it was normal practice for a pilot to scan his instruments – glancing at them rather than actively reading them – which on many occasions meant that the altimeter was misread. This was not so serious in larger, slower aircraft, like bombers and transports; but in fighters, which could dive at high speeds, the correct reading of clear and unambiguous instruments often meant the difference between life and death.

The Crash Site

Visiting the crash site of the Venom requires careful planning as it is very remote and the terrain difficult to traverse. However, in my opinion, it is one of the most worthwhile sites to visit. Apart from perhaps the Starfighter (see Chapter 18), it is one of the largest and most visible crash sites, with a substantial proportion of the aircraft still in situ. Much of the remains are piled up in a gully next to the fence but more may be found if you walk a few hundred metres down the hill. In fact, the wreckage (which includes parts of the engine, the wheel hub and part of the ejector seat) may be plotted along the last known line of flight.

Russell Gray

10

Fairey Flycatcher Is N9677 and N9679

Aircraft Type:	**Fairey Flycatcher I**
Serials:	N9677 and N9679
Codes:	14 (N9677) and 13 (N9679)
Unit:	No 404 Flight, HMS *Courageous*
Base:	NOT KNOWN
Crew:	Pilots: both unidentified
Crash Date:	23rd and 24th April 1930
Crash Location:	Falstone, North Tynedale, Northumberland
Grid References:	80/717872 (N9677) 80/718875 (N9679)

The Aircraft

Designed to Specification N6/22 for a single-seat biplane fighter to replace the ageing Nieuport Nightjar, the Fairey Flycatcher was one of the first aircraft specifically designed to operate from aircraft carriers. Three prototypes were built (N163–5), each one representing a different configuration: landplane, floatplane, amphibian. The design was of mixed wood and metal construction with fabric covering, and was very robust. The wings, which were of short span to facilitate stowage aboard aircraft carriers, featured a novel camber-changing mechanism to aid deck-flying operations; and the whole aircraft was designed to be easily dismantled, with no section longer than 13 feet 6 inches.

The first Flycatcher prototype to fly was the landplane (N163) on 28th November 1922, followed by the floatplane (N164) in May 1923. Power was provided by an Armstrong Siddeley Jaguar 14-cylinder piston engine, and both versions were judged an immediate success. Service trials on land and at sea were conducted early in 1923 and led to orders for 192 Flycatcher Is which were produced from 1923–30.

Flycatcher N9679 in the pasture, following its initial forced landing, undergoes repairs. (I. Wright)

Flycatcher Is entered service with No 402 Flight of the Fleet Air Arm in 1923 and went on to equip Flight Nos 401–409 and No 801 Squadron (ex-No 401 Flight) which operated from the decks of aircraft carriers and catapults atop gun-turret platforms on some capital ships. Few official documents from that period still exist, so information pertaining to the two Flycatcher Is involved in the accidents are sparse. However, thanks to the work of renowned aviation historian Ray Sturtivant, some details of their respective histories are known.

N9679 first entered service with No 401 Flight in February 1924. Thereafter it appears to have been stationed with various shore-based establishments before joining No 404 Flight aboard HMS *Courageous* by May 1928. N9677 similarly appears to have had a chequered early career, but unlike N9679, much of its service appears to have been at sea. It first joined No 402 Flight aboard HMS *Eagle* in 1926 before joining No 404 Flight aboard HMS *Courageous* in July 1929.

HMS *Courageous* was constructed in 1916 by Armstrong Whitworth on the banks of the River Tyne in Newcastle. Originally commissioned as a battle-cruiser, she was later recommissioned at Devonport as a fleet carrier and was launched as such in 1928. The carrier immediately set sail and spent the next two years patrolling the Mediterranean. During this time, two Flights of Fairey Flycatcher Is served aboard the carrier: No 407 Flight (May 1928 to November 1931) and No 404 Flight (May 1928 to November 1932).

HMS *Courageous* returned to British waters on 30th January 1930, arriving at Portsmouth before departing for Devonport on 8th February for a refit. During this time its two Flycatcher Flights departed for various bases in the south of England, including Croydon in Surrey and Gosport in Hampshire.

The Crashes

On 22nd April 1930, Flycatcher Is N9679 (coded 13), N9677 (14) and N9917 (8) of No 404 Flight took off from Croydon at the start of a flight to the naval air base at Donibristle in Fife. As the three aircraft approached central Northumberland, N9679 started to experience engine trouble and a decision was made to attempt a forced landing in a valley below. However, due to the high ground in the area, and the fact that there were lambs in the fields, it proved difficult to find a suitable landing place. Despite this the pilot managed to land his aircraft on a rough incline at High Yarrow Pasture just to the west of Falstone. Having confirmed that both pilot and aircraft were safe, the two remaining Flycatcher Is continued on to Donibristle.

The pilot of N9679 wired Donibristle for spares and the following day, at around 10.00 hours, N9917 and N9677 returned to High Yarrow Pasture with the necessary parts. First down was N9677, which attempted to land beside N9679 in the rough pasture, but the Flycatcher bounced badly causing the undercarriage to collapse and the aircraft crashed, thankfully without injury to the pilot. Having witnessed N9677's misfortunes, the pilot of N9917 wisely decided not to risk a landing in the pasture and instead chose the field at the foot of Yarrow Bank. Although the field was small and difficult to negotiate due to the roof tops of Yarrow and its tree-lined boundaries, the pilot carried out a successful landing.

N9917 took off at again at 12.15 hours, having dropped off the spares, and N9679 was duly repaired. Despite the rough terrain and the new obstacle of N9677 sitting nearby, N9679 successfully took off again; but it soon became apparent that the engine was knocking badly. The pilot had

Flycatcher N9679 following its second forced landing, with the buildings of Yarrow behind. (M. Massham)

The plane seen after its failed take-off attempt from the field. (I. Wright)

no choice but to make yet another forced landing, this time in the field at the foot of Yarrow Bank, and this was a success. The aircraft was repaired for a second time and yet another take-off was attempted, but the pilot failed to gain sufficient speed and struck the fence at the eastern boundary of thc field. The aircraft ended up on its nose with a smashed propeller and shaft; the pilot was uninjured.

The Aftermath

Both N9677 and N9679 were later salvaged and transported by road to Donibristle, where they were later repaired and returned to service.

Surveying the scene today, it is clear that the pasture chosen by the pilot of N9679 for his initial forced landing was a less-than-ideal place in which to put the aircraft down. The ground has a relatively steep incline and the terrain is uneven, which suggests that he had little time to make a decision on where to land. Given these facts, it is therefore surprising that this same location was chosen by the pilot of N9677, who did not experience any difficulties with his aircraft and had time to pick his landing spot; all the more so given the fact that the second returning pilot, flying in N9917, chose the field at the foot of Yarrow Bank, and made a successful take-off from it later that afternoon.

***Local resident Alastair Murray standing on the same spot in 2005.* (J. Corbett)**

It appears that a catalogue of errors and downright bad luck played their part in the demise of both Flycatchers. What a way to welcome the first aircraft to land in North Tynedale!

The Crash Sites

Except for the addition of Kielder Reservoir, the area where the forced landings took place has changed very little since April 1930, so locating the two crash sites from contemporary photographs was a relatively easy task as the field boundaries are exactly as they were in 1930. Because both Flycatchers were salvaged for repair, it was no surprise that not a trace of either aircraft could be found at the two crash sites when we visited the scene in October 2005.

Jim Corbett

11

Handley Page Hampden I L4054

Aircraft Type:	**Handley Page Hampden I**
Serial:	L4054
Code(s):	NOT KNOWN
Unit:	No 83 Squadron, RAF
Base:	RAF Scampton, Lincolnshire
Crew:	Pilot: Pilot Officer Wilfred Roberts Navigator: Pilot Officer Keith Brooke-Taylor Wireless Operator: Aircraftman 1st Class Denis W. Sharpe Observer: Sergeant Andrew McNicol
Crash Date:	7th April 1940
Crash Location:	400 metres inland of St Mary's Island, Whitley Bay, Tyne and Wear
Grid Reference:	88/343753

The Aircraft

In September 1932 the Air Ministry issued Specification B9/32 for a twin-engined bomber, and design proposals were duly accepted from two aircraft manufacturers with considerable experience in bomber design: Vickers (Type 271) and Handley Page (HP52). Both designs, though noticeably different, were built as prototypes of what would become the Vickers Wellington (see Chapter 29) and the Handley Page Hampden; two of the three twin-engined medium bombers (the third was the Armstrong Whitworth Whitley; see Chapter 1) that entered service during the expansion and re-equipment of RAF Bomber Command in the pre-war years.

Both the Wellington and the Whitley stemmed from a desire for larger aircraft able to carry a heavier bomb load. By contrast the Bristol Blenheim, which entered RAF service in 1937, sacrificed payload for performance. The Hampden – faster and more manoeuvrable than the Wellington and Whitley but with a smaller payload; slower than the Blenheim but with almost double the payload and range – was somewhere in the middle; a compromise between these two philosophies.

The prototype HP52 (K4240) flew for the first time on 21st June 1936, powered not by Rolls-Royce Goshawks as first envisaged, but by more powerful Bristol Pegasus P.E.5S(a) nine-cylinder radial engines. The aircraft was unusual in appearance, notable features being the slim tail-boom, highly tapered wings, twin tail and a complete absence of any power-operated gun turrets. Maximum speed was 254 mph.

The Air Ministry, impressed by the results of the early flight tests, placed an initial order for 180 Hampden Is within six weeks of the first flight. The first production aircraft (L4032) flew on 24th June 1938 and it, along with the second example (L4033), went to the Aeroplane & Armament Experimental Establishment at Martlesham Heath in Suffolk. Production in England eventually totaled 1,270 Hampden Is, with a further 160 built in Canada.

The third production aircraft (L4034) became the first Hampden I to enter service with RAF Bomber Command when it was assigned to No 49 Squadron at RAF Scampton in Lincolnshire in September 1938. By the end of that year, No 49 Squadron and No 83 Squadron were fully equipped with Hampden Is.

Once in operational use, the Hampden I failed to live up to its early promise. Of particular concern was the ineffective defensive fire provided by six .303 calibre machine guns mounted in the nose (one fixed, one moveable) and the dorsal and ventral turrets (two each). The nose-mounted .303s were all but useless; the two turrets had limited traverse and notable blind spots. In addition, the four-man crew endured cramped accommodation that quickly induced fatigue. The result was that the Hampden proved to be extremely vulnerable to enemy fire; a fact brought home when losses began to mount during daylight raids that started on 4th September 1939.

The Hampden squadrons were soon switched to night-time operations that included leaflet raids and mine laying, the Hampden I being the first RAF Bomber Command aircraft to sow mines in enemy waters. Better

A Handley Page Hampden.

defensive armament along with armour plating and flame-damping exhaust shrouds were introduced in an attempt to reduce still further the type's vulnerability, but fundamental shortcomings meant that it had a comparatively short operational career with Bomber Command that ended with a raid on Wilhelmshaven by No 408 (Goose) Squadron, Royal Canadian Air Force, on the night of 14th/15th September 1942.

The Hampden soldiered on with RAF Coastal Command, which operated Hampden TB1 torpedo bombers against German shipping in the North Sea. This variant featured a deepened bomb bay able to carry a single torpedo, and equipped three squadrons that were detached from Bomber Command in the summer of 1942 until the arrival of Bristol Beaufighters in late 1943.

The Crash

Hampden I L4054 of No 83 Squadron took off from RAF Scampton at 19.15 hours on the evening of 6th April 1940 for a 'security patrol' and offensive operations in the district of Sylt and north-west Germany. At the controls was Pilot Officer Wilfred Roberts (Service No 40319). Born in Brisbane, Australia, but educated in New Zealand, Roberts had embarked for Great Britain on 14th August 1937. After completing his flying training he was awarded his pilot's badge on 28th April 1938 and was then posted to No 83 Squadron at RAF Scampton on 22nd October 1938, where he converted onto the Hampden I.

Denis Sharpe. (courtesy of the Sharpe family)

Crashed 7th April 1940

In the navigator's seat was Pilot Office Keith Brooke-Taylor. Born in Wellington, New Zealand, he headed for Great Britain in July 1938 to undertake his flying training, after which he joined No 185 Squadron at RAF Thornaby in Yorkshire on 9th June 1939 to fly Avro Ansons and then Hampdens. During October he was posted to No 83 Squadron. In February 1940 the squadron proceeded to RAF Lossiemouth in Morayshire, from where he flew four operational sweeps over the North Sea and then returned with the squadron to RAF Scampton in March 1940.

Aircraftman 1st Class Denis Sharpe, a former grocer's assistant from Leicester, joined the RAF on 14th May 1937 and upon completion of his basic training became a wireless operator. By December 1938, Sharpe had been posted to No 83 Squadron and in 1939 he volunteered as an air gunner. He was promoted to Aircraftman 1st Class on 1st December 1939. Unfortunately, little is known about Sergeant Andrew McNicol.

At 22.10 hours the pilot of another aircraft, at an altitude of 5,000 feet and about one mile north of Sylt, saw some enemy searchlights centred on an unidentified aircraft well below him. He witnessed a great deal of tracer fire directed towards the aircraft and assumed that it must be L4054, no other aircraft having reported being fired upon that night. The instructions were to maintain wireless transmission silence at all times except in an emergency. The aircraft was heard twice through the night, however, once at 21.49 hours and again at 21.53 hours, asking Heston for call signs.

Nothing more was heard from L4054 until it appeared in the vicinity of St Mary's Lighthouse at 02.45 hours, where we believe it circled for about 1½ hours, repeatedly signaling SOS on a lamp; but an eyewitness to the crash, Mr Colin Bell, who was manning the searchlight at the time, has suggested that it may have circled for considerably less time, perhaps as little as 10-15 minutes. This was confirmed at a later date by another witness, Mrs A. Crisp. The SOS was challenged by the then lighthouse keeper, Mr Harold Owen Hall, who, after receiving the correct reply, immediately contacted the appropriate authorities. No Morse signal other than the SOS was picked up from the aircraft.

The standard procedure to aid lost aircraft – and one which would certainly have been familiar to Pilot Officer Roberts – was to train searchlight beams over a wide area towards the nearest RAF base equipped to receive a stricken aircraft. In this instance the beams were trained towards

RAF Acklington, which lit its flare path at 03.00 hours. Instructions on how to find the base were transmitted to the Hampden by Morse lamp, the signal reading: 'St. Mary's Lighthouse, follow the beam for Acklington'. Each word was acknowledged by a dash on the Hampden's signalling lamp, but Pilot Officer Roberts made no attempt to follow the searchlight beams. The Hampden continued to circle and was even seen to come down low as if attempting to land; in fact the landing light was seen to be in use. Eventually one engine appeared to fail and shortly after 04.00 hours three of the crew abandoned L4054 by parachute. These men were all drowned. The fourth member of the crew remained inside the Hampden, which crashed at 04.21 hours approximately half a mile from St Mary's Lighthouse. The aircraft was blown to pieces by its own bombs, leaving a crater some 25 feet in diameter and 15 feet deep. Mrs Crisp who lived on the island described the explosion as looking like a poplar tree.

The Aftermath

The official RAF team assigned to investigate the crash of L4054 concluded that, because Pilot Officer Roberts disregarded instructions to fly to RAF Acklington, this suggested that he was aware that the aircraft was damaged in such a way as to render a landing hazardous. The fact that none of the bombs were jettisoned over the North Sea would indicate that the bomb-bay doors or bomb-release mechanism were damaged. The report also concluded that the wireless operator, Aircraftman 1st Class Sharpe, remained with the aircraft because he was unable to leave it, having been badly wounded or killed. The wireless silence from 21.53 hours tends to support this theory.

The RAF investigation concluded that L4054's hydraulic system had been so badly damaged that the crew could not lower the undercarriage or open the bomb-bay doors. It would have been too dangerous to attempt a belly-landing at RAF Acklington, therefore it was deemed wiser to remain in a known area until daylight and then safely evacuate the aircraft.

I believe this to be a simplistic conclusion. While I can accept the view that the Hampden's hydraulic system was damaged to such an extent that to attempt a belly-landing provided an unacceptable risk, the events took place at night in early April and the waters of the North Sea would have been extremely cold. Given these conditions, to have deliberately parachuted over the sea seems to me to have been extremely foolhardy, with a very high probability of being washed offshore and dying of exposure.

The obvious course of action would have been to parachute over land, leaving L4054 to fly on out to sea, but this was not done. One can only assume that the pilot, even though he was very experienced, had become disorientated and was no longer aware of where the sea and land were. Perhaps he was not even aware which country he was over; after all, the crew had been flying alone at night for many hours over a black sea using navigation methods that were somewhat rudimentary so early in the war.

Whatever the reason behind the decision of the three crewmen to parachute when they did, it turned out to be the wrong one. Exactly what happened in their final hours now rests with them. We can only wonder about the tensions and emotions and what dramas were acted out in the black sky over Whitley Bay on that night in April 1940.

The Crash Site

As with many aircraft searches, the best place to start was with the farmer who owns the land on which L4054 crashed. Therefore I decided to contact David Thompson, who gave me permission to search and also advised me where to look. This we did with enthusiasm and immediately began to discover war-related finds in the fields, especially bullets. However, these had to be dismissed as being from L4054 because the area had also been used as a firing range by the Army during the war.

In the meantime I contacted Morag Horseman, chairman of the Friends of St Mary's Lighthouse, and she in turn directed me to the daughter of the then lighthouse keeper, Patricia Gumbrell, whose father witnessed the crash of L4054 and helped the RAF with their original investigation. This also confirmed, as if any confirmation was needed, that the aircraft did in fact crash on land and not in the sea, as so many people believed.

Morag persuaded me to publish the story of the loss of L4054 and its crew on the internet as part of the World Lighthouse Society's newsletter. Doing this was to change the whole complexion of the search because Maureen Wheelhouse, who was desperate to find out more about the death of her uncle, Aircraftman 1st Class Denis Sharpe, the wireless operator on L4054, read the article and made contact. It was then that I discovered that Denis's sister, Barbara, was still alive and anxious to know more. Maureen and Barbara decided to come up to the crash site and help with the search. We were about to enter the next chapter of this dramatic story.

The authority to recovery any remains from L4054 will never be granted by the Ministry of Defence, because it cannot be confirmed that all of the bombs exploded on impact. However, with members of Denis's family present it was decided to try to find any surface remains of the crash. So on 12th September 2007, ACIA members – watched by Morag Horseman, Barbara, and Denis's nieces Maureen, Pat and Jennifer – began to scan the fields with metal detectors in order to find anything remotely aviation-orientated and to conduct a comprehensive survey of the fields around the island so as to determine the position of the crash. After two hours of intensive field-walking using metal detectors and the 'Mk 1 eyeball', we began to find shards of Perspex, lumps of molten aluminium and twisted fragments of aluminium, indicating that we had indeed come across the crash site. These discoveries were actually reinforced at a later date by an eyewitness who was woken by the crash and went to see it the following day, but was stopped from doing so by military guards.

It was very dramatic and moving to find remains of Hampden L4054, most notably for the family of Denis Sharpe, the only member of the four-man

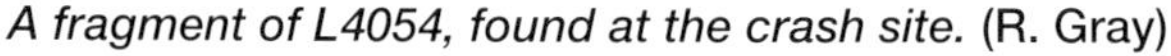

A fragment of L4054, found at the crash site. **(R. Gray)**

***The crash site today. An ACIA volunteer marks potential finds.* (R. Gray)**

crew whose body was not found after the crash. As more bits and pieces of L4054 were recovered, there was an especially poignant moment when part of a folding compass or ruler was found; it may even have belonged to Denis himself. The search continued all day in the hot sun and it was decided to make plans for some form of memorial to the dead airmen, possibly with a guard of honour supplied by the RAF Association.

It is always a fitting end to a search for the remains of an aircraft when family members achieve closure on the fate of their relatives; and this was true for the family of Denis Sharpe, who were even able to apply for and receive the medals he was entitled to. Barbara never knew anything about her brother's fate other than that he was missing on operations. His death certificate even has him 'lost at sea'! Now, though, we know a lot more.

A decision to honour these four brave airmen was quickly made and arrangements for a memorial tribute were soon in hand. A brass plaque was commissioned by the Sharpe family and a date as close to the anniversary of the crash was deemed appropriate for the ceremony. This took place inside St Mary's Lighthouse on 12th April 2008. Many local dignitaries were invited, including the commanding officer of RAF Boulmer who unveiled the plaque. A guard of honour was arranged by No 1156 (Whitley Bay) Squadron, Air Training Corps and a flypast by a Sea King search and rescue helicopter from RAF Boulmer opened the ceremony. Some two years of work had come to fruition and emotions ran high, especially for the Sharpe family, who were now able to bring to a close a lifelong search to find out what had really become of their dear brother and uncle. The plaque is now a permanent fixture in the lighthouse and will remain there in memory to the courage of the crew of Hampden I L4054.

Russell Gray

The guard of honour that attended the memorial service in 2008.

12

Hawker Hunter F6A XG236

Aircraft Type:	Hawker Hunter F6A
Serial:	XG236
Code(s):	N
Unit:	No 66 Squadron, RAF
Base:	RAF Acklington, Northumberland
Crew:	Pilot: Flying Officer Bryan Schooling
Crash Date:	14th February 1958
Crash Location:	Wainhope, Kielder Forest, Northumberland
Grid Reference:	80/674935

The Aircraft

The Hawker Hunter, Great Britain's most successful post-war fighter (1,972 were built) and promoted as 'the finest fighter aircraft in the world', was one of the RAF's first true multi-role jet aircraft. It was developed from the Hawker P1067, a prototype built in response to Air Ministry Specification F3/48 which called for a swept-wing fighter with a level speed of Mach 0.94, flight endurance of one hour, and radar ranging for either four 20mm or two 30mm cannons. The engine was to be one Rolls-Royce Avon or Armstrong Siddeley turbojet.

Three prototypes were built of the P1067, which could trace its lineage back to Hawker's first jet-fighter studies in late 1944, the first of which (the Avon-powered WB188) flew on 20th July 1951. Some four months earlier, with US and Soviet jet fighters involved in combat over Korea on an almost daily basis, a contract had been placed for 113 production Hawker Hunters and the project given 'super priority' status.

The first production Hunter F1 (WT555) flew on 16th May 1953; but this model was plagued by engine problems, particularly when the cannons were fired, and difficulties associated with operating at high subsonic speeds. Finding solutions to these problems delayed the F1's entry into service with RAF Fighter Command until July 1954. Two months later, in September, the first of 45 Hunter F2s entered service.

The Hunter F1 and F2 were short-range interceptors, their flight endurance limited by a lack of fuel. This was addressed in the Hunter F4 and F5, with increased internal fuel capacity and the ability to carry auxiliary drop tanks on two of four underwing pylons which could also be used to carry bombs, rockets or rocket projectiles, thus giving the Hunter a dual-role day-fighter/ground attack capability. A detachable gun pack positioned beneath the cockpit now contained four 30mm cannons.

These expanded capabilities were incorporated into the Hunter F6, flown in P1099 prototype form (XF833) on 22nd January 1954. Improvements included a more powerful Avon 203 engine, which gave the F6 a maximum speed of 715 mph and an initial rate of climb of 17,200 feet per minute, and modifications to the wing and tail for better handling and manoeuvrability. A combination of the Hunter's beautiful streamlined shape and the improved handling characteristics made the F6 a popular aircraft with pilots; and 383 were built (more than any other Hunter model) for service with RAF squadrons in Great Britain, Germany and Cyprus.

The first production Hunter F6 (WW592) flew on 25th March 1955 and the new model entered operational service with RAF Fighter Command's No 19 Squadron at RAF Church Fenton and No 66 Squadron at RAF Linton-on-Ouse, both in Yorkshire, in October 1956. By 1958, all of the RAF's day-fighter squadrons had been re-equipped with Hunter F6s. However, as with earlier Hunter models, the F6's operational service life was comparatively short; and by November 1962 it had been replaced by the Lightning F2. A small number of Hunter F6s received some of the Hunter FGA9's equipment fit and were known as Hunter F6As. Another 126 F6s underwent the full conversion to FGA9 standard for service with the RAF in the ground attack role.

Hunter F6A XG236 was built under Contract No 10345 by Hawker Aircraft Ltd at their Kingston upon Thames factory in October 1956, and was part of the third production batch of 110 aircraft. It was test-flown by Duncan Simpson on 19th October, and by 8th November was ready for collection by the RAF. The next day, XG236 was issued to No 5 Maintenance Unit,

Crashed 14th February 1958

Hunter XG236 wearing Iraqi Air Force markings en route to Baghdad in 1957. (A. Aked)

a holding unit at RAF Kemble in Gloucestershire, before allocation to an operational squadron. At this time RAF Kemble still had many new Hunter F4s, and it was not until 28th November that XG236 was issued to No 66 Squadron.

In May 1957 No 66 Squadron went on detachment to RAF Akrotiri in Cyprus. Whilst there, XG236 and another of the unit's Hunters were flown to Baghdad in Iraq to act as standby aircraft for a flypast of brand new Iraqi Air Force Hunters. Both aircraft had their RAF roundels painted over with the Iraqi Air Force's triangular insignia, but they retained their existing squadron codes. Shortly after No 66 Squadron's return from Cyprus, the unit moved north from RAF Linton-on-Ouse to RAF Acklington in Northumberland, where it stayed until it was disbanded in 1960.

The Crash

At 09.07 hours on 14th February 1958, Flying Officer Bryan Schooling took off from RAF Acklington in Hunter F6A XG236 and climbed away at the start of a local aerobatic exercise. Born in Battersea in London on 18th August 1934, Schooling's childhood interest in becoming a fighter pilot was fuelled by watching wartime air battles over Surrey, which led him to enlist in the RAF in 1952. Following pilot training at the RAF College at

Cranwell in Lincolnshire, Pilot Officer Schooling was commissioned on 13th December 1955 and posted to No 145 Squadron at Celle in Germany.

Schooling remained with No 145 Squadron until it was disbanded on 27th October 1957, by which time he had been promoted to Flying Officer. On 5th November he joined No 66 Squadron at RAF Acklington, just over a year after the squadron had replaced its Hunter F4s with the superior Hunter F6, making it only the second RAF Fighter Command squadron to operate the new variant. His first flight in the Hunter F6 took place on 8th November 1957, but his subsequent flying training was severely disrupted by poor weather conditions over the north-east of England. Nevertheless, on 8th February 1958 he returned from a month-long Instrument Rating Examiner course at RAF West Raynham in Norfolk with an 'above average' assessment.

Prior to take-off on the morning of 14th February, Schooling attended the daily weather briefing, then went to No 66 Squadron's crew room to be briefed on what was to be the first flight of the day. The weather was poor, with rain and low cloud forecast for most of the region. With visibility of half a mile or less, the use of instruments would be essential when flying through

Bryan Schooling, far right, poses with fellow pilots whilst serving with 145 Squadron at RAF Celle in Germany. **(Family of Bryan Schooling)**

cloud. Schooling was also authorised for local flying practice with inboard drop tanks fitted. The flight briefing called for him to climb to 25,000 feet. However, in order to break cloud and enter clear air, it is assumed that he climbed an additional 15,000 feet.

At 09.12 hours, five minutes after Schooling's departure, two pairs of Hunters took off for Battle Formation Flying. They broke cloud at 33,000 feet, but due to the lack of a visible horizon, both pairs climbed another 5,000 feet. The Hunters then began their exercise and had been doing so for about five minutes when, out of nowhere, they were 'attacked' by a lone Hunter carrying inboard drop tanks. The leader countered the attack by turning and diving steeply into cloud, which was 7,000 feet below. The attacking Hunter was about 500 yards behind him when he selected airbrakes out and recovered from his dive on instruments, levelling out at 22,000 feet at a speed of just over Mach 0.9.

At 09.28 hours Walter Beattie was tending to his stock on the 324 acre farm of Wainhope, part of the recently planted Kielder Forest, when he heard the sound of an aircraft flying very low and fast in the clouds overhead. The noise was followed immediately by the sound of a loud explosion from the hillside to the north. Local postman, David Daley, was in Plashetts when he heard the aircraft and then a thud, bang and whine. Wainhope was the last stop on his round and on reaching the farm he was informed by Walter what had happened. He immediately returned to Plashetts to raise the alarm.

At the same time, RAF Acklington was trying to re-establish contact with Flying Officer Schooling in XG236, after all contact had been lost. At 10.10 hours Acklington was informed that an explosion had been heard in the Bellingham area, and by 10.30 hours a helicopter had been scrambled to search an area north of Plashetts Station. In the meantime, forestry workers had made their way up to the crash site. They were busy searching for signs of the pilot when the helicopter was seen to fly overhead, circle some distance away and then fly off.

One of the first on the scene was Dennis Summers, a forestry worker from Plashetts, who arrived to find a hole 40 feet long and 20 feet deep in which pieces of wreckage were still burning. Due to the severity of the crash, many small fragments of the aircraft were scattered for nearly half a mile beyond the point of impact in the direction in which XG236 had been travelling.

By 11.05 hours police and a fire appliance were on their way from Bellingham to the scene of the accident, and at 12.28 hours RAF Acklington was informed that the pilot's body had been located in the wreckage. Later the aircraft was identified by its survival equipment as Hunter F6A XG236. By 12.50 hours a No 275 Squadron Bristol Sycamore helicopter was on its way from RAF Ouston in Northumberland with a medical officer on board to recover the remains of the pilot.

The RAF recovery team spent several days recovering the wreckage of XG236 from the bog, during which time the compacted remains of the Avon engine were winched out of the crater. Due to the boggy nature of the terrain, much of the crumpled wreckage was left at the foot of the deep crater. Despite the use of water pumps, the recovery team were beaten back by the water which constantly flowed back into the hole, and so the salvage was abandoned.

The Aftermath

The accident was subject to a Board of Inquiry during which a study of the radar film for the period confirmed the attacking aircraft as Hunter F6A XG236. Among the Board's findings was evidence that the aircraft had 30 degrees of flap down and airbrakes in when it crashed. It was also established that the canopy was in place at the time of impact, which confirmed that Flying Officer Schooling had made no attempt to eject. The aircraft struck ground at a height of 1,200 feet, when the cloud base in that area was 1,000 feet, so it was noted that the pilot was in cloud almost from the moment he entered his dive until the moment of impact.

The Board considered that when Schooling carried out the unauthorised attack, he quickly reached a speed at which elevator control became inadequate. To recover from such a position in cloud whilst on instruments would have been difficult. The final conclusion was entered on the Form 1180 (Crash Card) as follows: 'The pilot was directly responsible for the accident in that he carried out an unauthorised attack on another aircraft, and followed it into cloud using 30 degrees of flap in a high-speed dive. He then became disorientated and failed to regain control on instruments.'

There was a Mach 0.9 limit on the use of Hunter flaps. RAF records state that the Hunter that was the subject of Schooling's attack took evasive action by diving steeply and then recovered by applying airbrakes and levelling out at just over Mach 0.9 at 22,000 feet. If XG236 was in pursuit 500 yards behind, the dive it entered might have exceeded a speed of Mach 0.9.

When it becomes necessary to turn an aircraft within its minimum radius, as in a dogfight, it is common practice to use a small amount of flap to enhance the lift from the wings, thus giving a better turning performance. It is possible that Flying Officer Schooling had lowered XG236's flaps for this purpose, but forgot to raise them again once he had entered the dive. In such a high-speed dive and in cloud it would have been quite easy to become disorientated. This, combined with the problem with the Hunter's flaps, made recovery almost impossible.

In 1963, following a spate of Hunter accidents, the RAF carried out an investigation into the phenomena of what became known as elevator jack stall and tailplane actuator clutch slip. Several accidents formed the basis for this investigation, one of them being the loss of XG236. Prior to 1963, the RAF was aware of a problem with the use of the Hunter's flaps at high Mach, but did not yet fully understand the cause.

With the technical evidence from the inquest stating that XG236 had 30 degrees of flap down when it crashed, it must be assumed that the loss of tailplane effectiveness, highlighted in the 1963 test programme, was a major contributing factor in the loss of this aircraft. When control is lost in such circumstances, recovery action must be immediate and can only be achieved by raising the flaps and reducing speed.

The fact that Flying Officer Schooling was a relatively inexperienced Hunter pilot must also be taken into account. At the time of his death he had accumulated only 50 hours on type, only three of which were in the previous month. Therefore it seems harsh to place direct responsibility for the accident on a pilot who was not only inexperienced on type, but who also may not have been fully aware of its quirks – especially its erratic behaviour with flaps down at high Mach.

The Crash Site

ACIA's plan in the autumn of 2007 was to attempt to locate the wreckage of XG236, buried deep within the crater, to establish the orientation of the aircraft at the point of impact. The suggestion was that the Hunter hit the ground in an inverted position, so locating the compacted cockpit and

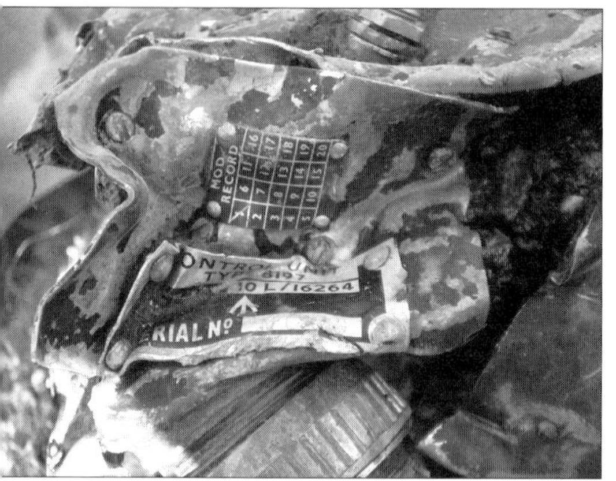

Wreckage is still being uncovered at the crash site. **(J. Corbett)**

The partly drained crater following the dig in 2002. **(J. Corbett)**

front fuselage may hold the key as to whether Flying Officer Schooling was in control of the aircraft when it crashed.

The crash site is situated on private Forestry Commission land approximately one mile north of Wainhope, in an area of recently felled and replanted trees. Here a large, water-filled crater clearly marks the point of impact, with some small pieces of the aircraft scattered in the vicinity. Excavations at the site in June 2001 and 2002 meant that the crater had to be drained, which revealed large amounts of wreckage to a depth of approximately 15 feet.

The Hunter crashed at a steep angle on a heading of 253 degrees; on impact it continued in the direction of travel for another half-mile. A furrow on the eastern side of the crater indicates that a substantial part of XG236 struck the ground just prior to the main impact, which suggests that the dive was not as steep as the Board of Inquiry first thought. Forestry worker David Armstrong recalled that a member of the RAF team sent up to investigate the crash stated that the aircraft was inverted on impact. The position of various components unearthed during ACIA's excavation of the crash site supports this claim.

Jim Corbett

13

Hawker Hurricane IV KX190

Aircraft Type:	**Hawker Hurricane IV**
Serial:	KX190
Code(s):	B
Unit:	No 1 Specialised Low Attack Instructors School, RAF
Base:	RAF Milfield, Northumberland
Crew:	Pilot: Flight Sergeant John Gates
Crash Date:	22nd June 1943
Crash Location:	Steng Moss, one mile SSE of Elsdon
Grid Reference:	80/951915

The Aircraft

The Hawker Hurricane, design of which began in 1934 as the 'Fury Monoplane' and later the 'Interceptor Monoplane', was a private venture to meet the requirements of Air Ministry Specification F5/34 (later revised as Specification F36/34). The result was the first eight-gun monoplane to enter service anywhere in the world; and the first RAF fighter to exceed 300 mph. During the course of the Second World War the Hurricane served in every major theatre of conflict in a variety of roles that included day-fighter, night-fighter, fighter-bomber, tank-buster and catapult fighter.

The prototype (K5083) flew on 6th November 1935 and quickly earned a reputation for excellent performance and handling. The Air Ministry, impressed by what it saw, placed an initial order for 600 production Hurricane Is in June 1936, and the first of these (L1547) flew on 12th October 1937. Powered by the Rolls-Royce Merlin II, the first examples went to No 111 Squadron at RAF Northolt in Middlesex in December 1937, thus heralding the end of the biplane fighter in RAF service.

By September 1939, when war broke out, 497 Hurricane Is had been delivered and equipped eighteen squadrons – twice as many units as had Spitfires. On 7th August 1940, generally accepted as the start of the Battle of Britain, 2,309 Hurricane Is had been delivered and equipped 32 squadrons (enough Spitfires had been delivered to equip nineteen units).

***A Hurricane Mk IV, with its under-wing cannons.* (J. Gates)**

The Hurricane II first flew in June 1940 and was powered by the Merlin XX. As with the Spitfire, different armament combinations were reflected in the Mk designations: Mk IIA (eight .303 calibre machine guns); IIB (twelve .303s); IIC (four 20mm cannons). Other features included a tropical air filter (for desert operations), self-sealing fuel tanks and under-wing auxiliary fuel tanks.

The addition of under-wing bombs produced the 'Hurribomber'; but it was the fitting of two 40mm guns (with two .303s for ranging) and up to eight rocket projectiles that gave the Hurricane a new lease of life as the Mk IID optimised for tank-busting in the desert. This led in turn to the Hurricane IV, externally almost identical to the Hurricane II from which it was derived, and the only RAF fighter specifically armoured with a ground-attack role in mind. An additional 360 pounds of steel armour plate protected such areas as the cockpit, engine nacelle and radiator from flak and ground fire.

The Hurricane Mk IV's 'universal armament wing' could carry a wide range of external stores such as rocket projectiles (eight), 500-pound bombs (two), 40mm anti-tank guns (two) and long-range fuel tanks (two plus one beneath the fuselage). Once the weight of this ordnance was added to that of the wingfour 20mm cannons (armament), the aircraft's handling was markedly different to that of its predecessors. Because of the substantial increase in weight, the Mk IV was fitted with the more powerful 1,620 hp Merlin XX engine.

By mid-1944 the Hurricane IV had been entirely replaced by the Hawker Typhoon in the European theatre, but it continued to be used extensively in the Far East with six squadrons equipped until the end of hostilities. The last examples soldiered on in Palestine until January 1947.

Hurricane IV KX190 was built by Hawker at their Langley factory on 2nd January 1943. The aircraft was first issued to No 5 Maintenance Unit at RAF Kemble in Gloucestershire where it was kitted out with operational equipment and then, on 5th January 1943, issued to No 1 Specialised Low Attack Instructors School (No 1 SLAIS) based at RAF Milfield in Northumberland, where it was used to train the new wave of ground attack fighter pilots for the RAF.

The Crash

On the morning of 22nd June 1943, Flight Sergeant John Gates took off from RAF Milfield for a low-level cross-country exercise. Accompanying him in a second Hurricane was his No 2, Warrant Officer Albert Witham. John Gates enlisted in the Royal Australian Air Force on 15th August 1941. All of his early training was carried out in Australia, after which he left for Great Britain on 24th August 1942. He arrived on 18th November and was transferred to No 17 Pilots Advanced Flying

F/Sgt John Gates. **(J. Gates)**

Unit at RAF Bodney in Norfolk, arriving there on 9th February 1943. Exactly a month later he was transferred to No 59 Operational Training Unit (OTU) at RAF Milfield, where he began training on Hawker Hurricanes.

During his time with No 59 OTU, Flight Sergeant Gates must have shown some promise as a ground-attack pilot, because on 19th May he was posted to No 137 Squadron at RAF Manston in Kent, designated as a ground-attack squadron. Despite his new posting he was retained at RAF Milfield but transferred to No 1 SLAIS, which was operating Hurricane IVs, the type also being flown by No 137 Squadron at that time. With No 1 SLAIS Gates would hone his skills in ground-attack techniques, carrying out low-level sweeps over the bombing ranges at Goswick and Doddington North Moor and simulating attacks on moving convoys.

The purpose of the exercise on the morning of 22nd June was to carry out a low-level sweep of the area south of the base and a camera-gun attack on any Army vehicles encountered in the area. The two Hurricanes headed south, following the Vale of Wooler before turning south-west over Hepple and heading into the Grasslees Burn Valley. Keeping near to the valley floor the Hurricanes encountered a ridge of high ground ahead which they successfully passed over. On the other side of the ridge, and immediately ahead, they spotted a convoy of Army vehicles heading east along a road at a right angle to their intended flight path. Flight Sergeant Gates opened up his camera-gun and began a diving attack on the vehicles, passing so low that he struck the radio aerial on one of them.

Climbing away, Gates performed a stall turn to the left to enable him to carry out a second attack. By this time the convoy had stopped in a small dip in the road. Gates had just pulled his Hurricane level when it struck rising ground just to the south of the road; the rise caused the aircraft to bounce over the convoy, missing the vehicles by a matter of feet, and then cartwheel out of control on the northern side. The Hurricane broke apart on impact and the wings, tail and engine all became detached from the forward fuselage. By the time the aircraft stopped moving, the only identifiable piece that remained was the battered cockpit with Gates trapped inside.

The captain in charge of the Army unit set off across the rough ground half-expecting to find a mangled corpse trapped in the wreckage. To his surprise he heard Flight Sergeant Gates shouting that he was alive but that his feet were trapped under the rudder bar. With the help of others from the convoy, the cockpit was righted and Gates was pulled clear. Although still alive, he had suffered a serious injury to his left arm, as well as numerous abrasions and shock. He was immediately transferred by ambulance to Newcastle General Hospital where he spent the next two months, during which time it was established that his left arm was paralysed as a result of injuries sustained. Gates was then transferred to Winnick Emergency Hospital in Warrington, a specialist nerve treatment unit, for further treatment to his left arm.

No 137 Squadron pilots in front of a Typhoon. John Gates is in the middle row, 5th from left. **(J. Colton)**

The Aftermath

So what caused the crash of Hurricane IV KX190? John Gates recalled that the aircraft reacted sluggishly when he tried to pull it out of the dive; and that despite having the throttle fully open, it struck the ground just as it was beginning to pull level.

Gates had previously flown earlier marks of Hurricane whilst with No 59 OTU; but although they were almost identical in physical appearance to the Mk IV, they lacked the latter's additional 360 pounds of steel armour plate. This additional weight, combined with a lack of experience on type, almost certainly played a crucial part in the accident. If it were not for the rising ground just to the south of the convoy, the outcome could have been far worse, for it was this that caused the Hurricane to bounce over the Army convoy and not into it, which would almost certainly have killed or maimed Gates and those Army personnel inside the vehicles.

Flight Sergeant Gates eventually made a full recovery and, after finishing his training with No 1 SLAIS, returned to service and joined

No 137 Squadron on 21st September. Later he was promoted to Flying Officer and transferred to ground-attack Hawker Typhoons. Whilst flying a Typhoon over Germany on 5th December 1944, his aircraft was struck by flak which damaged the flight controls and set the cockpit alight. Flying Officer Gates was knocked unconscious during his attempt to bail out of the stricken Typhoon and when he came to he found that he was falling towards the ground. He managed to deploy his parachute just in time, but the subsequent landing was a heavy one. Gates was captured by a German army unit and spent the last months of the war in a prisoner-of-war camp. He was eventually liberated by General Patton's advancing US forces.

The Crash Site

To the untrained eye there are no obvious signs of the events of 22nd June 1943; the area of the crash looks no different to other stretches of moorland in the area. However, hidden in the undergrowth within a few yards of the road, some small pieces of Hurricane IV KX190 can still be found.

Jim Corbett

The general area of the crash site with the road in the distance. The cannons were wedged in the stone dyke in the foreground. **(J. Corbett)**

Hawker Tempest V EJ859

Aircraft Type:	**Hawker Tempest V**
Serial:	EJ859
Code(s):	NOT KNOWN
Unit:	No 56 Operational Training Unit, RAF
Base:	RAF Milfield, Northumberland
Crew:	Pilot: Flight Lieutenant Vincent Parker
Crash Date:	29th January 1946
Crash Location:	Felkington Farm, Northumberland
Grid Reference:	939449

The Aircraft

Designed to Air Ministry Specification F10/41, the Hawker Tempest was a development of the same company's Typhoon (see Chapter 15) which had disappointed as a fighter, with a poor rate of climb and only modest performance at altitude. The Typhoon went on to excel as a fighter-bomber, but the need for a capable fighter-interceptor remained.

In an attempt to solve the problem the Tempest featured a new, aerodynamically improved wing to enhance performance. The wing was thinner and could hold less fuel than that of the Typhoon, so the Tempest's fuselage was lengthened to accommodate extra tank capacity. Three different engines were used on different models, but only the Napier Sabre and Bristol Centaurus were selected for production models, namely the Tempest V (Sabre) and Tempest II (Centaurus).

Two prototype Mk Vs were ordered in November 1941, powered by the Sabre VI and Sabre II respectively. Even before the first prototype, a converted Typhoon (HM595), flew on 2nd September 1942, the Air Ministry had placed an initial order for 400 production Tempests, the first of which

A Hawker Tempest Mk V prototype.(www.raf.mod.uk Crown Copyright)

(JN729) took to the air on 21st June 1943.

The Tempest V, 805 of which were built, was powered by the 1,820 hp Sabre II and retained the Typhoon's distinctive beard air-scoop. It was the only version to see wartime service and made its operational debut with No 486 Squadron (part of the first Tempest Wing) at RAF Newchurch in Kent in January 1944. Six months later, as the first of the V1 flying-bombs dropped on southern England, the Tempest V, with a maximum speed of 435 mph and armed with four 20mm cannon, led the aerial fight to intercept and down these 'revenge weapons' on what were known as anti-'Diver' patrols. The fighter's success can be gauged by a simple statistic: Tempest Vs downed 638 out of the 1,771 'doodlebugs' that were destroyed by the RAF between 13th June and 5th September 1944.

In addition to the four cannon carried in the wings, Tempest Vs could carry up to 2,000 pounds of bombs or eight rocket projectiles, each of the latter fitted with a 60 pound warhead. These weapons enabled the Tempests, which now equipped eleven operational squadrons, to play a key role in support of Allied ground forces as they advanced through north-west Europe after the D-Day landings. The Tempests also took on the threat posed by German jet fighters, using their speed to catch and down twenty Messerschmitt Me 262s as the Luftwaffe made its last stand.

The Tempest V continued to serve the RAF in the post-war years, using its impressive speed to great effect as a target tug. The last examples were retired from service as late as July 1955.

The Crash

At 14.00 hours on 29th January 1946, Flight Lieutenant Vincent 'Bush' Parker took off from RAF Milfield in Northumberland in Tempest V EJ859 to take part in a camera exercise. By 14.30 hours the 27-year-old pilot lay dead amidst the wreckage of his aircraft scattered in a Northumberland field.

Vincent Parker was born Vincent Wheatley on 11th February 1918 in Chester-le-Street, County Durham. His surname was later changed to that of his maternal aunt and uncle, with whom he emigrated to Australia in 1927, his mother having died when he was four years old. In early 1939 the threat of war and a desire to fly with the RAF brought him back to these shores.

Having earned his flying licence at the Civilian Flying School at Gatwick, which gained him entry into the RAF, his training began in August 1939 with No 11 Fighter Training School at RAF Shawbury in Shropshire, where he gained his pilot's badge on 25th October. Pilot Officer Parker was posted to No 234 (Madras Presidency) Squadron at RAF Leconfield in Yorkshire on 10th April 1940, which was in the process of re-equipping with Spitfires and gaining experience as a fighter unit.

F/Lt Vincent Parker.

His first real sortie was on 13th May 1940 when a section of 'B' Flight, consisting of three aircraft, was sent up at 17.05 hours to intercept an unidentified aircraft. No interception was made and the three Spitfires returned to base 30 minutes later. Parker was back in the air twice on 28th May; he intercepted a Whitley bomber on the first but nothing on the second. These must have been tense times for the pilots, running to their aircraft not knowing what they might find in the air, but also exhilarated to be doing the job for which they had trained.

Vincent Parker is seated centre on the right wing in this group picture of No 234 Squadron.

Pilot Officer Vincent 'Bush' Parker was one of 'The Few' who fought in the Battle of Britain, but his luck ran out on 15th August. Scrambled at 17.05 hours from Middle Wallop in Hampshire, to which his unit had moved that day, he and his colleagues were tasked to patrol Swanage in Kent and counter the then-biggest force the Luftwaffe had sent against Great Britain to attack not only the south coast but also north-east England. By the end of the day the RAF had lost 34 aircraft, the Luftwaffe 71. Vincent was one of four pilots from No 234 Squadron who were shot down that day, but he managed to bail out over the English Channel without injury. He was rescued not by friendly forces but a German E-boat, and was taken to Cherbourg and then on to Germany as a prisoner of war.

RAF officers were expected to do what they could to harass the enemy and escape whilst imprisoned and Parker tried to escape from the German E-boat, only to be re-captured. His efforts continued during his time in captivity as POW 476, starting at the Dulag Luft interrogation centre and ending at Oflag IVC – Colditz Castle. It was here, on 16th April 1945, that he was liberated when American forces managed to break through and storm the area. During his time in captivity he was still eligible for promotion, so it was Flight Lieutenant Parker who was released and repatriated to Great Britain, then sent to No 56 Operational Training Unit at RAF Milfield in Northumberland in December 1945.

The Form 1180 (Loss Card) for the crash of Tempest V EJ859 states that the aircraft appeared to commence a slow roll at 5,000–6,000 feet but that, when in the inverted position, its nose fell and the Tempest descended in a slow spin. Parker managed to effect a recovery at approximately 100 feet, but the Sabre engine stalled and the aircraft crashed into a willow tree before hitting the ground at Bakers Bog on Felkington Farm. His death was RAF Milfield's last recorded casualty before it closed down operationally at the end of the Second World War.

Vincent Parker (second from right) with fellow prisoners, including Douglas Bader (centre, with pipe) on liberation day at Colditz.

The Aftermath

Flight Lieutenant Vincent 'Bush' Parker was Mentioned in Despatches on 13th June 1946, some four months after his death. It is safe to say that his duty as an RAF pilot during the Battle of Britain and his subsequent activities and prowess during his time as a prisoner of war were more than enough to grant him this honour. He died at the age of 27, the day before the anniversary of his mother's death. Fate had decreed that they both die young. Vincent is still remembered and missed by his family in Australia as well as Great Britain, and will remain so for many years to come.

The Crash Site

The land is still owned by the family that bought it in 1950, some four years after the fatal accident. Cameron Martin was an eight-year-old boy when his dad bought the farm, but he can remember a six-foot hole in Bakers Bog and the split trunk of a willow tree. Now, some 58 years older and a farmer on the land, he can still remember the location of the hole which has been transformed from a bog into a plantable crop area; but a visible gap in the hedgerow (where the willow tree stood) still exists, a small depression marking the trunk of the tree.

Neil Anderson

15

Hawker Typhoon IB MN140

Aircraft Type:	**Hawker Typhoon IB**
Serial:	MN140
Code(s):	NOT KNOWN
Unit:	No 609 (West Riding) Squadron, RAF
Base:	RAF Acklington, Northumberland
Crew:	Flying Officer Charles Detal
Crash Date:	23rd March 1944
Crash Location:	North Seaton, Northumberland
Grid Reference:	81/298868

The Aircraft

The Hawker Typhoon, with its large and distinctive air-scoop, tremendous firepower and great speed at low level, proved to be an exceptionally successful ground-attack aircraft armed with bombs, rocket projectiles and 20mm cannons; but it was actually designed to meet Air Ministry Specification F18/37 which called for a single-seat high-performance fighter-interceptor armed with twelve .303 calibre machine guns. The Specification stated that production aircraft would be built around the powerful Napier Sabre or Rolls-Royce Vulture engine; as a result, two prototypes of each of two designs from Hawker were built: the Type 'N' (Typhoon) and the Type 'R' (Tornado).

The Type 'R' prototypes (P5219 and P5224) flew on 6th October 1939 and 5th December 1940 respectively, and the RAF placed an initial order for 500 production Tornados. However, neither the aircraft nor its engine lived up to expectations, and when Rolls-Royce cancelled production of the Vulture in 1941 the plans to acquire Tornados were dropped.

Hawker Typhoon IB MN140

Crashed 23rd March 1944

The first Sabre-powered Type 'N' (P5212) flew on 24th February 1940. Once again the RAF placed orders for the production Typhoon I – and once again problems came to light during flight-testing. The Sabre engine proved to be unreliable and it soon became clear that the Typhoon would not be a suitable replacement for the Spitfire or Hurricane as an interceptor due to its slow rate of climb and poor performance at heights above 20,000 feet. It did, however, prove to be an extremely impressive gun platform, and performed well at low level.

The first production Typhoon IA (R7576) flew on 27th May 1941 and deliveries to RAF squadrons commenced in September that year, the first examples going to No 56 Squadron at RAF Duxford in Cambridgeshire. This sudden rush into service was largely due to the introduction of the FW 190 into Luftwaffe service; an extremely fast and versatile fighter/fighter-bomber that RAF Fighter Command found it could not match.

The haste with which the Typhoon was introduced turned out to be an error and many early aircraft were lost due to problems with the elevators, incapacitation of the pilot by exhaust fumes entering the cockpit, and structural failure of the tail assembly. Production was halted for a time so that the factories could concentrate on building Hurricanes while the Typhoon's problems were ironed out.

Production of the Typhoon IA, armed with twelve .303 calibre machine guns, ended after only 105 had been built, replaced by the Mk IB with four 20mm cannons. By the end of 1942, Typhoons were being armed with two bombs for use against enemy shipping and airfields; and the introduction of rocket projectiles in late 1943, up to eight of which could be carried, revealed the Typhoon's deadly capabilities as a 'train-buster'. The Typhoon, 3,317 of which were built, had developed into a highly successful fighter-bomber which, at its peak, equipped 26 squadrons of 2nd Tactical Air Force.

Typhoon IB MN140 was delivered to No 51 Maintenance Unit on 4th January 1944. The Form 78 (Movement Card) for the aircraft states that it was subsequently issued to No 486 Squadron (date unknown) before moving to No 197 Squadron on 31st January. By March 1944 it had again been transferred, this time to No 609 (West Riding) Squadron. Exactly when MN140 joined this unit is unclear, but on 23rd March it was flying out of RAF Acklington in Northumberland, to where some of that squadron's aircraft had just moved for training.

The Crash

Flying Officer Detal DFC, seen here while serving with 609 Squadron. **(via A. Bar)**

Shortly after midday on 23rd March 1944, the first anniversary of his joining the unit, Flying Officer Charles Detal, DFC, took off from RAF Acklington in Northumberland in Typhoon IB MN140 for practice attacks over the range at Druridge Bay. These exercises were designed to improve the ground attack skills of aircrew in the build-up to the Normandy landings, and involved aircraft attacking targets in the water and on the beach, while a controller observed the results from a bunker in the sand dunes.

Born in Profondeville in Belgium on 28th March 1914, Detal joined the Belgian Air Force in 1934 and by the outbreak of the Second World War was serving with 5th Flotilla (Blue Eagle) unit. After recovering from serious injuries sustained when he was shot down on 29th May 1940, Detal successfully managed to escape from Belgium into Switzerland and then on to France. From there, with help from (amongst others) the famous Pat O'Leary escape line, he managed to make his way over the Pyrenees and into Spain. He reached Portugal in early 1942, and on 11th April 1942 finally landed in Great Britain, where he joined the Belgium Section of the RAF.

After a conversion course, during which he would have been introduced to RAF procedure and the Typhoon, Detal was posted to No 609 Squadron on 23rd March 1943. During his time with the unit he was involved in a great number of operations and was credited with 5½ enemy aircraft destroyed in the air, 2½ destroyed on the ground, and 2 damaged on the ground. His last operational flight was on 15 March 1944 when he took part in a defence patrol in Typhoon IB JR192. Six days later he moved with twelve other of the squadron's Typhoons to RAF Acklington.

As he and his partner that day, Flying Officer Polo Cooreman, waited for their turn to attack the targets in Druridge Bay, Detal became bored and slightly frustrated and decided to carry out a mock dogfight with his colleague. Closing in to less than 1,000 feet in a tight turn, Detal lost control and MN140 spun towards the ground. Although he managed to recover from the spin, the Typhoon had lost too much height and crashed into a field about 300 yards north of North Seaton Hall.

The whole incident was witnessed by Tommy Laidlaw, a young lad from Newbiggin-by-the-Sea who was helping to plough the field known as Broad Meadow with a pair of horses, when he and the men he was working with spotted three aircraft. At first they thought the trio were German Messerschmitts because they had square wing-tips, but as they came closer, Tommy and the others realised they were friendly. Tommy and the other men assumed the aircraft were going to attack a number of old tanks that had been placed on Newbiggin Golf Course, but then one of the aircraft seemed to lose control. Tommy recalled how it dived towards the ground, and how the pilot only managed to regain some control very close to the fields, by which time it was too late. As the Typhoon levelled out, still travelling very fast, it hit the ground and collided with trees on the edge of the road known locally as Summerhouse Lane, and came to rest in the field opposite the one in which Tommy was working, which belonged to Nellis's Farm. The body of the pilot was apparently some 20 yards away from the aircraft, having been thrown clear on impact.

The Aftermath

The official inquiry stated that the turn carried out by Flying Officer Detal had been too tight while the Typhoon was carrying practice bombs, and that the increased weight load on the wings as a result of the manoeuvre had caused the aircraft to go into a spin. If the aircraft been at a higher altitude, Detal might have survived (he had managed to pull out of the dive), but unfortunately he was killed on impact. After recovery, Detal's body was transported to London where it was laid to rest at Brookwood Cemetery; but after the war it was exhumed and returned to Detal's native Belgium and re-interred.

Thus, through a flying error during training, another brave airman died many miles from his home. With some 1,045 flying hours (213 of which were on Typhoons), over 100 operational flights and 5½ confirmed aerial victories, the loss of such a senior member of No 609 Squadron was a great blow to the unit and the men he flew with, especially for the fellow Belgian pilots with whom he had served.

The Crash Site

Typhoon MN140 crashed on fields after almost managing to recover from a dive and came to rest by the trees on the edge of Summerhouse Lane. The fields are now playing fields. (J. Shipley)

There is little evidence at the crash site today of what happened on that day in March 1944. The reports stating that the pilot had managed to pull the aircraft out of the steep dive prior to the impact would account for the aircraft hitting the ground at a shallow angle, which stopped the Typhoon from burying itself deep in the ground. While the field that eyewitness Tommy Laidlaw was in when he watched the aircraft's final moments is still used for arable farming, the area where MN140 finished her final flight is now used as playing fields.

Jonathan Shipley

16

Heinkel He 111H-5 3550

Aircraft Type:	**Heinkel He 111H-5**
Serial:	3550
Code(s):	A1+CK
Unit:	2./KG53, Luftwaffe
Base:	Virty-en-Artois, France
Crew:	Pilot: Unteroffizier Karl Rassloff Navigator: Gefreiter E. Lernbass Wireless Operator: Unteroffizier Karl Simon Mechanic: Gefreiter W. Schmidt Air Gunner: Gefreiter H. Quittenbaum
Crash Date:	6th/7th May 1941
Crash Location:	St George's Hospital, Morpeth, Northumberland
Grid Reference:	81/204872
	Gefreiter = Lance Corporal Unteroffizier = Sergeant

The Aircraft

Designed in 1934 in response to a joint Deutsche Lufthansa/German Air Ministry requirement for a high-speed commercial transport and a medium bomber, the Heinkel He 111 was an enlarged development of the single-engined He 70 *Blitz* (Lightning) four passenger mail-carrier. The He 70 was both fast (it set nine world speed records in 1933) and versatile, its airline service complemented by military versions used for light bombing and long-range armed reconnaissance.

The prototype He 111a first flew on 24th February 1935, and over the following months several variations of the new 'airliner' were tested by the

A Heinkel He111 in flight, taken from the cockpit of another He111. Note the large Perspex front section of the aircraft. **(J. Shipley's collection)**

Luftwaffe. During 1936 the He 111C entered service with Deutsche Lufthansa as a ten-seat transport, but the real focus was on development of a bomber fit for front-line service. A change of engine in 1936 proved to be the key to success as it provided the levels of power necessary for the He 111 to operate at operational weights with a respectable bomb load.

Combat experience gained in the Spanish Civil War (as part of the famous Condor Legion) led to various improvements in engine power, fuel capacity, bomb load, armour protection and defensive armament. The He 111H, which featured the recently introduced and highly distinctive asymmetric glazed nose, was the most successful and prolific of all the bomber models, with some 800 in service at the beginning of the Second World War. A host of improvements and refinements were incorporated in numerous sub-variants, including the Jumo 211-powered H-5 which had external racks for bombs or torpedoes, increased fuel capacity, better armour protection for the five-man crew, and defensive armament of up to seven 7.9mm machine guns and one 20mm cannon.

The Crash

On the evening of 6th May 1941, approximately 380 German bombers took off from bases throughout Europe to attack targets in Great Britain. Their main target was the Clydeside/Glasgow area which was attacked by 232 aircraft, 155 of which focused their attack on the Greenock to Dumbarton area. Between 00.10 and 02.45 hours the force dropped a little over 170 tonnes of high explosives, along with 38,750 incendiaries,

Crashed 6th/7th May 1941

W/Op Karl Simon, and the pilot Karl Rassloff standing in front of an He111, with two mechanics. **(Karl Simon via Bill Norman)**

while the Glasgow area received some 97 tonnes of high explosives and 2,304 incendiaries. Other targets attacked included Newcastle, Liverpool and Plymouth; however the Luftwaffe lost some twelve aircraft during the night, four of which crashed on British soil.

At about 11.50 hours, He 111H-5 3550 approached the north-east coast of England on its way to Dumbarton. Unknown to its five-man crew, the bomber's presence had been detected by Flying Officer Day and Pilot Officer Lanning in Boulton Paul Defiant I night-fighter N1796, operating with No 141 Squadron out of RAF Acklington in Northumberland. Day managed to position the Defiant beneath the lumbering German bomber; then Lanning, the gunner in the Defiant's power-operated turret, fired three short bursts from his four .303 calibre Browning machine guns from a distance of about 100 feet. Before the German crew knew what had happened the bomber's port engine had been disabled, which then set fire to the wing.

As the stricken bomber lost altitude, its crew seemingly did not realise the extent of the damage and changed course, heading out to sea. The wireless operator, Unteroffizier Karl Simon, radioed his base at Virty-en-

The crash site, shortly after He111 H-5 3550 crashed at Morpeth. After coming to a stop at the edge of Bluebell Woods, the front section burnt out, leaving the rest of the fuselage and most of one wing intact. (via Ken Watkins)

Artois in France and stated that they were returning with one engine damaged; however it soon became clear that they would not make it back. In a letter to the author Bill Norman, Simon told of how control and supply leads had been damaged, while the fire caused oxygen bottles that supplied the breathing equipment to explode and blow a hole in the fuselage.

As the situation aboard the bomber deteriorated, it was decided that they should land in Great Britain. Simon radioed a second message to base informing them that they would not be returning, shortly after which the pilot made a perfect belly-landing in the grounds of St George's Hospital in Morpeth. The bomber skidded across the field in a shower of sparks observed by the Defiant's crew, and came to rest with the forward fuselage section hitting trees in what is known locally as Bluebell Woods. As fire took hold, the bomber's crew made their way out of the burning aircraft, and sheltered against a nearby hedge where they were found by a male nurse from the hospital who had witnessed the crash. After first being held at the hospital, the crew were removed to Morpeth police station from where they were collected by an RAF Intelligence Officer.

The fire raged on for over 45 minutes after the crash, destroying the forward section of the fuselage and one of the wings; but it was eventually extinguished by a fire crew from Morpeth. In the days that followed, the site was investigated and cleared by an RAF recovery team who also had the difficult job of guarding the site.

Crashed 6th/7th May 1941

The crash-landing of a German bomber in the north was not a common occurrence, and children from Morpeth were quickly at the site to look for souvenirs. Mr MacKay of Morpeth was one of the children to visit the site, and managed to retrieve a pocket watch, while others salvaged molten aluminium and pieces of Perspex. One young man working as a messenger for the fire service was even able to rescue one of the machine guns, but this was later recovered and the boy fined.

After the recovery, large sections of the aircraft were put on display throughout the north, including Manchester, Liverpool and Hull, the last stop being Newcastle, where it is believed the remains of the aircraft were scrapped. However, James Davidson, who was born in Morpeth, recalls that the undercarriage wheels remained on the site and were subsequently removed to Hewits Garage in Morpeth in the 1950s when he was a teenager.

The Aftermath

For the crew of the Defiant, He 111H-5 3550 was not their only 'kill' that night. After refuelling at RAF Acklington they took to the air again and downed a second German bomber, this time a Junkers Ju 88A-5, which crashed on Holy Island, the crew also being taken prisoner. Both Day and Lanning were awarded the Distinguished Flying Cross.

Day's life was cut short some three years later on the afternoon of 18th June 1944, when his flight of Spitfires from No 132 (City of Bombay) Squadron ran into six FW 190s over the Fécamp-Evreux area of France. Day's Spitfire IX (ML120) was hit by flak while he chased one of the German fighters, and large parts of the rudder were lost. His last radio message stated that he was at 5,000 feet, which would have been a safe height at which to bail out, but nothing more was heard from him. It remains unclear whether he died whilst bailing out or in the resulting crash. His body now lies in Connelles Churchyard, the only Commonwealth War Grave in the cemetery.

Frank Lanning survived the war, and in the years that followed joined the Control Commission established to run post-war Germany. Following this he worked in the Diplomatic Service before going into publishing, and on retiring he moved to Darlington where he died in 2002 a week before his 95th birthday.

The Crash Site

Bluebell Woods are quiet once again, and are popular with dog-walkers and youngsters alike. No obvious evidence remains of the dramatic events that occurred on that night in May 1941, apart from a gap in the trees caused by the impact of the forward fuselage. The field the bomber skidded over before coming to a halt is now home to the new St George's Hospital. However, small fragments of burnt aluminium still litter the area around the base of the trees, and dark burnt earth marks the area where the He 111 was consumed by flames.

Jonathan Shipley

The site today – the gap in the tree line caused when the plane crashed is still very clear, although the small field that it skidded over prior to coming to a halt is now a wing of St George's Hospital. (J. Shipley)

Small pieces of burnt and molten aluminium, along with a piece of burnt rubber and small fragments of copper, mark the site where the front section of the He111 burnt out in May 1941. (J. Shipley)

17

Junkers Ju 88A-4 1064

Aircraft Type:	**Junkers Ju 88A-4**
Serial:	1064
Code(s):	4D+BD
Unit:	Stab III/KG30
Base:	Aalborg, Norway
Crew:	Pilot: Oberfeldwebel Helmut Riede Navigator: Oberfeldwebel Rudolf Elle Wireless Operator: Oberfeldwebel Helmut Dorn Air Gunner: Feldwebel Walter Müller
Crash Date:	1st September 1941
Crash Location:	Bedlington Brickworks, Bedlington, Northumberland
Grid Reference:	81/273834
	Feldwebel = Sergeant Major Oberfeldwebel = Warrant Officer

The Aircraft

The Junkers Ju 88, by far the most versatile German warplane of the Second World War, originated to meet a requirement issued in early 1935 for a three-seat high-speed bomber with a maximum bomb load of 1,765 pounds and defensive armament consisting of one 7.9mm machine gun in the dorsal position. The requirement also stipulated demanding performance criteria, including a maximum speed of 310 mph.

Junkers began design work in January 1936, the team including two Americans, W. H. Evers and Alfred Gassner, who had considerable experience in the development and use of new stressed-skin construction methods. Construction of the first prototype, the Ju 88V1 (D–AQEN), began in May, and the aircraft took to the skies for the first time on 21st December 1936. The twin-engined aircraft was powered by Daimler Benz DB 600As and featured a heavily glazed pilot's cabin.

The design was tested and perfected over the next 2½ years using ten prototypes, notable changes including replacement of the DB 600As with Jumo 211As, the addition of a distinctive 'beetle's eye' glazed nose and a ventral gondola for a single 7.9mm machine gun, and provision for a fourth crewman.

The V-series prototypes were followed by ten pre-production Ju 88A-0s for service trials which began in early 1939; these were followed by the first production model, the Ju 88A-1, which entered service in September 1939, at the outbreak of the Second World War. Some 60 A-1s had been produced by the end of 1939, but in 1940 the production rate for the Ju 88 family (including night-fighter and reconnaissance versions) shot up to 300 per month.

The Ju 88A-2 introduced attachment points for assisted take-off rocket packs; the A-3 was a dual-control trainer. The A-5 (which preceded the A-4) was fitted with longer wings and a strengthened undercarriage, combat experience in the early months of the war having revealed that, although the Ju 88A could carry three times the bomb load originally specified, its short wingspan meant that the aircraft required longer-than-normal runways to take off when flying fully loaded; and the risk of structural failure had resulted in the type being deemed unsuitable for dive-bombing.

This picture of a Ju 88A-4 was taken in Norway in May 1945. **(J. Shipley)**

Then came the Ju 88A-4: the most important and numerous member of the Ju 88A family and the basis for a further fifteen A-series variants. Like the A-5, the A-4 benefited from lessons learned in combat, most notably in performance (Jumo 211J engines), bomb load (raised to a maximum of 4,400 pounds on internal and external racks), crew protection (increased armour plating) and defensive armament (various combinations of up to seven 7.9mm and 13mm machine guns in the nose, forward fuselage, rear cockpit and ventral gondola). The A-4 also featured the improvements first introduced on the A-5.

The Crash

On the night of 1st/2nd September 1941, Ju 88A-4 1064 took off on a bombing raid against Newcastle. (Although it was never bombed as heavily as cities such as London, Plymouth and Coventry, Newcastle and the north did suffer at the hands of the Luftwaffe bombers.) At the controls was pilot Oberfeldwebel Helmut Riede (aged 25) accompanied by navigator Oberfeldwebel Rudolf Elle (29), wireless operator Oberfeldwebel Helmut Dorn (27) and gunner Feldwebel Walter Müller (26).

As the bomber approached the north-east coast the German crew probably had no idea that their activities had already been detected, and that closing in on them was a Bristol Beaufighter IIF night-fighter of No 406 (Lynx) Squadron, Royal Canadian Air Force (RCAF). Formed at RAF Acklington in Northumberland in May 1941 as the first RCAF night-fighter squadron, it had initially operated with Blenheims, but during the following month had started to take delivery of Beaufighters. Fitted with nose-mounted radar called Airborne Interception (AI), these night-fighters were flown by a pilot who was directed onto the target by a radar operator and ground operator.

Since receiving its first 'Beaus', No 406 Squadron had been working hard to perfect use of the new radar technology. By September the squadron was still not operational; but at 21.15 hours on the first of the month, Beaufighter IIF R2336 was scrambled and took off with Pilot Officer Robert 'Moose' Fumerton in the pilot's seat, and Sergeant Pat Bing as radar operator. Because the AI equipment only worked over a relatively short distance, once airborne the crew were passed over to a Ground Control Interception (GCI) operator who, using plots from ground-based radar, directed them to their prey.

The Beaufighter was over the North Sea at about 22.00 hours when its AI radar picked up the Ju 88A-4 some 5,000 feet away. Fumerton

***Bedlington brickworks, with the drying shed in the centre. Note the end of the gardens on the left showing how close the bomber came to hitting the residential area.* (J. Dawson)**

continued to follow the radar plots from Bing and was able to close in on the enemy bomber until he saw it enter cloud ahead of him. Bing used the AI radar to track their prey in the cloud, while Fumerton manoeuvred the night-fighter into position below, so that when the Ju 88 reappeared the Beaufighter, still undetected, was beneath it and close enough for Fumerton to be able to positively identify the aircraft as an enemy bomber about to cross the coast near the mouth of the River Wansbeck at Cambois.

Fumerton closed to 100 yards, pulled back on the control column to raise the Beaufighter's nose, then opened up with its four 20mm cannons and six .303 calibre machine guns at a distance of just 50 yards. The effects of such powerful and accurate firepower were immediately evident: the Ju 88, on fire, fell away to port, crossed Cambois and headed inland. As Fumerton came in for his second and final attack, Müller opened up with a short burst of return fire, but it was to no avail. The second salvo from the Beaufighter was deadly, breaking off the Ju 88's tail section and sending the bomber diving towards the ground where it crashed on the drying sheds of Bedlington Station Brickworks at 22.11 hours. This short combat had provided No 406 Squadron with its first victory, and cost the lives of four young German airmen.

When an aircraft half-full of fuel and already ablaze impacts with the ground, there is only one outcome: an uncontrollable fire. The downed bomber burned fiercely for some three hours after it hit the brickworks, and Bedlington Auxiliary Fire Service struggled to control the flames. The situation could have been far worse had the aircraft not missed houses on Stakeford Road and Bridge Terrace, some fifteen to twenty metres away on the other side of the railway line. Pieces which had broken off from the bomber during its final dive were scattered over the 2½ miles between Cambois and Bedlington Station, while four of the bombs it had been carrying exploded in fields behind the Burnside Estate slightly to the east.

The Aftermath

***P/O Fumerton and Sgt Bing holding up a piece of the Ju 88 1064 that they shot down over Bedlington. This was the first victory for No 406 Squadron and the cross they are holding became the Squadron scoreboard.* (B. Norman)**

The next day a team of RAF recovery men arrived on site under the command of Flying Officer McKenzie (a Technical Investigation Officer) and Flying Officer Benson (an interrogation officer). It took most of the day to search the wreckage, and it was not until the early evening that the remains of the four German airmen were identified. Jim Purdy of Bedlington Station was a teenager at the time and recalled how their remains were laid out in the paint shop, which had become a temporary mortuary. This grim task continued for the next few days, until all that could be recovered of the crew had been removed from the site. Both Fumerton and Bing visited the site and removed one of the black crosses from the wreckage; it was to become No 406 Squadron's 'scoreboard'.

In the meantime, the tail section of the Ju 88 had been discovered at nearby West Sleekburn, where it had fallen after being shot away. This was removed to East Sleekburn Farm, from where it was due to be recovered by the RAF. Instead it was thrown into the mud of the River Sleek below the farm, but not before many people had their photo taken with panels from the tail. During the coming days, locals also recovered a large number of items from the aircraft that had been scattered over the fields, including oxygen bottles, compasses and the crew dinghy. Some three weeks later the most deadly find was made by workers cutting hay in a field to the east of the brickworks: a large bomb that must have been dropped or broken free from the bomber as it fell towards the ground, possibly with the other four that had exploded when the plane crashed.

After recovery of the wreckage of Ju 88A-4 1064, the remains of her four-man crew were removed and laid to rest in Chevington Cemetery, some fifteen miles north of Bedlington, and very near to RAF Acklington from where Fumerton and Bing had taken off on that fateful night. Alongside the four graves are those of over 50 other airmen who died during the Second World War, including men from No 406 Squadron and thirteen other German airmen.

The Crash Site

No evidence of what happened on that night in September 1941 remains today. The brickworks continued to operate well into the 1960s, but after their closure the buildings were demolished; the site is now the Barrington Industrial Estate, with a house known as the 'Birches' on the site of the drying sheds. There is a chance that the remains of the Ju 88's tail lie buried nearby in the mud of the River Sleek – if indeed they were buried there in the first place. The most obvious – and poignant – reminder of what happened that night has to be the four graves that lie in a corner of an English churchyard, their occupants far away from home.

Jonathan Shipley

The site of the brickworks today. Trees now line the edge of the railway line and disguise the trading estate that now stands where the Ju 88 crashed. **(J. Shipley)**

18

Lockheed F-104G Starfighter D-8337

Aircraft Type:	**Lockheed F-104G Starfighter**
Serial:	D 8337
Unit:	No 312 Squadron, Royal Netherlands Air Force
Code(s):	NOT KNOWN
Base:	Volkel Air Base, Netherlands
Crew:	Pilot: 2nd Lieutenant Martin Sasbrink Harkema
Crash Date:	12th April 1983
Crash Location:	Three miles west of Alwinton, Northumberland
Grid Reference:	NOT AVAILABLE

The Aircraft

In 1952, with the United States heavily engaged in the Korean War, a requirement was formulated for a single-seat high-speed interceptor superior in performance to the Soviet jet fighters being used by Communist forces against the US Air Force (USAF) over Korea. Lockheed's response was Project 242, initiated in late 1952, which led in turn to the F-104 Starfighter; one of the first combat aircraft capable of sustained supersonic flight at high altitude.

Lockheed's revolutionary design featured a short-span wing that was ultra-thin (a maximum of four inches), a high-set tail, and a slender fuselage built around a single General Electric J79 turbojet engine with afterburning. The equipment and weapons fit were kept to a minimum in an attempt to keep weight down and thus maximise performance. The first of two XF-104 prototypes flew on 4th March 1954, followed by seventeen YF-104 pre-production aircraft with the fuselage lengthened by over five feet.

Starfighter D-8337 at RAF Coningsby, taken immediately prior to take-off for its final flight. **(Dutch Air Force)**

The first production variant, the F-104A, flew on 17th February 1956 and entered USAF service in January 1958. The weapons fit was optimised for interception: one 20mm cannon and two Sidewinder air-to-air missiles. Further development led to the F-104C strike-fighter with in-flight refuelling; and the F-104B and -D two-seat combat trainers. Engine problems, a troublesome ejector seat and the high-performance fighter's unforgiving handling characteristics led to a series of loses, and the USAF reduced its planned orders from 722 to just 296.

The Starfighter's salvation lay in Europe, where a consortium of countries led by Germany saw it as the answer to their air forces' need for a new multi-role fighter with which to equip their air forces; and, in Germany's case, a means by which the country's aerospace industry could be regenerated through licensed production. The result was the F-104G, over 1,200 of which were built in Germany, Belgium, the Netherlands, Italy and the United States. (A further 409 were built as camera-equipped RF-104Gs and two-seat TF-104G trainers.)

The F-104G's fuselage and wing structure were strengthened to cope with the stresses of low-level flight; an enlarged tail fin was fitted for better stability; the avionics were greatly improved; and the weapons fit was boosted, with up to 4,000 pounds of external stores (including tactical nuclear bombs) being carried for low-level penetration missions.

Production of the F-104G in the Netherlands was undertaken by Fokker and D-8337 rolled off the Schiphol production line on 30th November 1964. This particular aircraft entered service with the Royal Netherlands Air Force (RNethAF) on 22nd March 1965, assigned to No 312 Squadron – the last RNethAF squadron to receive the F-104G – at Volkel Air Base on the outskirts of Uden. In all, 120 F-104Gs were delivered to the RNethAF (95 were built by Fokker at Schiphol, 25 by Fiat in Italy) between December 1962 and January 1966.

No 312 Squadron was the sole user of D-8337 during its service life, operating it in the tactical strike role. The only incident of note during that time was a taxiing accident at Volkel on 2nd October 1973. On 16th December 1981 D-8337 reached a landmark 3,000 flying hours; to celebrate this feat the aircraft was painted with the slogan 'Dusty, 3000 hrs still the best there is' across the fuselage sides. It is not clear when this paintwork was removed, but it certainly was not worn when D-8337 crashed in 1983, although a smaller version of the Dusty cartoon character had been retained on the fin.

The Crash

Operation 'Mallet Blow', held on the Otterburn Military Ranges in Northumberland, was an exercise organised by the RAF to provide realistic training for NATO aircrews tasked with attacking ground targets, and for defending fighter squadrons, communications and jamming personnel and surface-to-air missile (SAM) units. Two ranges were in use during these exercises: 'Charlie', made up of a mock airfield defended by several SAM sites; and 'Bravo', the interdiction range on which pilots attacked a bridge or one of more than 70 derelict vehicles scattered across the firing area.

At its height in the early to mid-1980s, 'Mallet Blow' took place four times a year and involved aircraft from countries such as Great Britain, the United States, Germany, the Netherlands, Denmark, Sweden and France. During one such exercise in 1984, a total of 139 sorties were flown over the ranges.

The first 'Mallet Blow' exercise of 1983 began on 11th April with the arrival at RAF Coningsby in Lincolnshire of aircraft from France and the Netherlands, the latter represented by F-104Gs D-8061 and D-8337 from No 312 Squadron at Volkel.

On 12th April 2nd Lieutenant Martin Sasbrink Harkema was tasked to fly D-8337 as wingman to D-8061 for an attack on the bridge in the 'Bravo' range. The two aircraft departed RAF Coningsby and formed up over the North Sea. A method of attack was chosen in which both aircraft would engage the target in formation at low altitude and high speed. Once close to the target, both aircraft would turn to starboard and climb to about 650 feet, during which time Harkema would switch position from one wing of his leader to the other. The purpose of this switchover was to give Harkema a better view of the target and also to keep his F-104G out of the slipstream of the lead aircraft.

At 11.10 hours the two F-104Gs were observed from the ground by the umpire, Flight Lieutenant J. B. Bowen, on a Rapier missile site at Observation Post 6. He saw the two Starfighters in close formation flying from the south over Observation Post 3, which was situated on top of Highspoon Hill. The operator of the Rapier unit locked on to D-8337, the nearest of the two aircraft, which was flying on the port wing of D-8061. Flight Lieutenant Bowen started to observe the tracking on the commander's sight and continued to do so as D-8337 dived towards the bridge. He saw the Starfighter pass over the bridge and then almost immediately pitch nose-up, quite suddenly, by about ten degrees, followed by an equally sudden pitch nose-down of about five degrees. This continued until the third pitch-up when the tail of D-8337, which was in a 'wings level' attitude, struck the ground at the top of a ridge of high ground immediately behind the target. The aircraft slid along the ground for about 200 feet before it broke up and exploded, showering wreckage over a wide area. No ejector seat was seen to fire from the aircraft.

A Sea King rescue helicopter was scrambled from RAF Boulmer on the Northumberland coast with a medical officer on board. On arrival at the crash scene the body of 2nd Lieutenant Sasbrink Harkema was found amidst the twisted wreckage of his Starfighter. Later that evening, an F-27 Troopship arrived at Newcastle Airport with an investigation team from the RNethAF; it left the following morning with Harkema's body on board.

All flying across the Otterburn Military Ranges was cancelled after the accident, to allow the investigation team to get to work and try to establish what had gone wrong. Flight Lieutenant Bowen's eyewitness statement was crucial to the investigation, which now focused on the unusual pitch-up and pitch-down movements of D-8337 just prior to the crash.

The Aftermath

The results of the investigation were given at an inquest held on 8th May 1984. The investigation centred on the F-104G's stall-prevention device, the Automatic Pitch Control (APC), which would engage a system known as the Stick Shaker to warn of an impending stall. If this warning was ignored, another system called the Stick Kicker would automatically push the nose of the F-104G down in an effort to gain more air speed and prevent a stall. This was a perfectly acceptable and effective safety measure – but not when the aircraft was flying at such a low altitude. In fact it was common for more experienced Starfighter pilots to override the APC by flicking a switch in the cockpit when flying on low-level sorties.

So what caused the Starfighter to stall? The aircraft was diving at an acceptable speed when it pitched up after passing the bridge on the 'Bravo' range. The investigation pointed to the fact that 2nd Lieutenant Harkema had not switched over to the starboard side of his leader as briefed when commencing his attack; in fact he was 2,000 feet behind and a further 60–100 feet lower. At an altitude of only 146 feet the Starfighter was lower than anticipated and became caught between the ground and the slipstream of the leader's aircraft, which by this time had already bombed the target and was now climbing and banking away.

Realising he was fast approaching a ridge of high ground, 2nd Lieutenant Harkema reacted by pulling hard on the stick and consequently brought D-8337 up too sharply, at which point it entered the slipstream of D-8061; this disrupted the airflow over the wings which in turn caused the Stick Kicker to activate. As a result, D-8337 nosed down towards the ground. Because D-8337 was already at such a low altitude, there was simply too little time for 2nd Lieutenant Harkema to react to the pitch downwards, and the aircraft struck the rising ground behind the target with fatal consequences for the pilot.

The investigators also suggested that a contributing factor, which may explain why the switchover was not carried out correctly, was that when the two aircraft formed up over the North Sea a build-up of sea salt formed on the windscreens of both aircraft, which may have resulted in 2nd Lieutenant Harkema losing sight of his leader. Whatever the cause, what is certain is that 2nd Lieutenant Harkema simply did not have enough altitude or time to react to the situation.

The Crash Site

Mike Farrer with the General Electric engine found almost a mile from the main crash site. (J. Corbett Snr)

Possibly one of the largest crash sites in the north of England, the wreckage of D-8337 is almost exactly as the investigators left it in 1983, with large sections strewn across the boggy ground. The complete rear fuselage and tail unit is still present at the initial point of impact, with No 312 Squadron's badge and the F-104G's serial number still clearly visible on the fin. Two access panels on either side of the fin are missing, the Stabiliser Servo Actuator having been disconnected and removed from within, almost certainly as part of the post-crash investigation.

From this point, scattered in a north-westerly direction for a further 280 yards, various large sections of D-8337 litter the area, some of the more identifiable parts including one of the main undercarriage legs with tyre, port and starboard sides of the cockpit, ejector seat, cockpit canopy, jet pipe from the engine, both wings and the port-side engine intake complete with the Dutch military roundel. Some 500 yards beyond the furthest extremities of the wreckage, and down the northern slope of the hill, are the battered remains of the General Electric J79-11F engine, which continued to bounce for some considerable distance before embedding itself into a marsh.

The wreckage of D-8337, which amounts to about 85 per cent of the aircraft, is scattered over a distance of nearly half a mile across extremely boggy terrain, which in itself gives some idea of the speed the aircraft was travelling at when it crashed.

Jim Corbett

Crashed 12th April 1983

The tail fin and rear fuselage showing the 312 Squadron emblem. (J. Corbett)

Jim Corbett Snr, with intake nacelle showing the Dutch Air Force roundel. (J. Corbett Snr)

The starboard side cockpit panel. (J. Corbett)

19

North American Mustang I AG617

Aircraft Type:	North American Mustang I
Serial:	AG617
Code(s):	NOT KNOWN
Unit:	No 4 (Army Co-operation) Squadron, RAF
Base:	RAF Clifton, Yorkshire (?)
Crew:	Pilot: Flying Officer John Fisher
Crash Date:	19th February 1943
Crash Location:	Hareshaw Head, near Bellingham, Northumberland
Grid Reference:	80/833903

The Aircraft

The North American Mustang, to which so many bomber crews of the US Eighth Air Force owed their lives when these 'little friends' provided fighter-escort duties deep into enemy territory, actually resulted from the RAF's early-war need for a suitable single-engined combat aircraft with the range to enable it to operate over mainland Europe. In January 1940 the RAF's requirement was outlined to North American Aviation (NAA), which was already conducting its own in-house fighter design work in the hope of bettering the Curtiss P-40, which NAA was expected to build under licence.

By making use of its existing design work, NAA designed, built and rolled out the first prototype of its sleek new fighter in just 117 days. Known as the NA-73X, it lacked an engine; something that delayed the first flight until 26th October 1940 when NX19998 took to the skies powered by an Allison V-1710 inline piston engine. The engine supply problems were eventually resolved, and production began against an initial order for 320 examples of what the British christened the Mustang I.

North American Mustang I AG617

Crashed 19th February 1943

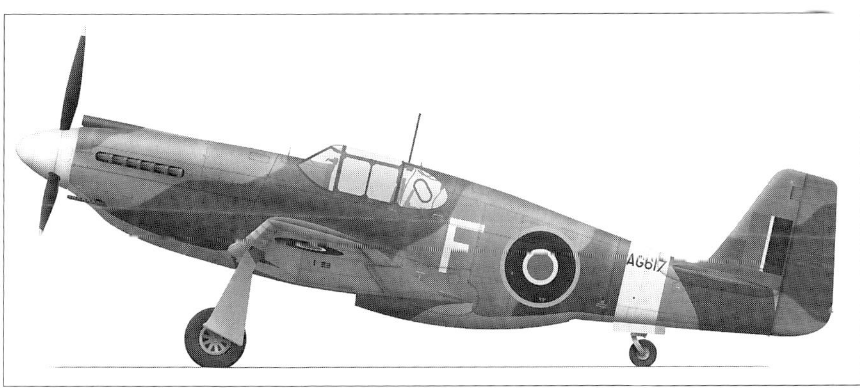

Artist's impression of a Mustang AG617. **(Simon Glancey)**

The first of the RAF's Mustang Is (AG346) flew on 1st May 1941 and arrived in Great Britain in October that year. The type's performance proved superior to any other US fighter at the time and even bettered the outstanding Spitfire V below 25,000 feet – maximum speed was 390 mph at 8,000 feet and it took eight minutes to climb to 15,000 feet; range was 1,050 miles and service ceiling was 32,000 feet – but in general the Allison engine's performance above 12,000 feet failed to meet expectations. Later models were powered by the Rolls-Royce Merlin 66 engine, and it was this change of power plant that enabled the Mustang to realise its full potential as a long-range fighter escort for Allied bombers operating far into Europe.

Because of its superior performance at lower altitudes, the Mustang I, 620 of which were ordered, was given the job of ground attack and armed tactical reconnaissance with 23 squadrons in the RAF's Army Co-operation Command. Armament consisted of four .303 and two .50 calibre machine guns in the wings and two .50s in the forward fuselage. A change in armament to four 20mm cannons and the addition of self-sealing fuel tanks distinguished the next model, the Mustang IA, 150 of which were ordered; and it was to this configuration that most Mk Is were built and delivered to Great Britain, after which they were modified to take the British .303/.50 armament combination. Both models could be fitted with a single F24 oblique camera in the port side of the fuselage, behind the cockpit.

On 19th April 1942, Mustang I AG617 arrived in Great Britain aboard the cargo ship SS *Laurity Swenson*. The aircraft was taken to Southport, probably for re-assembly, and then passed on to No 20 Maintenance Unit at RAF Aston Down in Gloucestershire for modification to Mk I standard with British armament. On 3rd February 1943 AG617 was finally taken on charge by No 4 (Army Co-operation) Squadron based at RAF Clifton near York. Unfortunately the aircraft's operational life only lasted just over two weeks.

The Crash

On 19th February 1943, Flying Officer John Fisher took off from RAF East Moor in Yorkshire in Mustang I AG617 for a flight to Edinburgh. Fisher was a former top pupil at Leith Academy Secondary School who had won a scholarship in Mechanical Engineering (with aeronautics as the main subject) at Glasgow University and Glasgow Technical College in 1938. From there he proceeded to No 3 British Flying Training School at Miami in Oklahoma. On his return from the United States, Fisher went to RAF Old Sarum in Wiltshire for training in his eventual role in No 4 (Army Co-operation) Squadron.

The entry in No 4 Squadron's Operational Records Book does not list a destination station for Flying Officer Fisher's flight, which leads us to speculate that this was a surprise visit to John's family who lived at Leith near Edinburgh. Sadly, AG617 mysteriously crashed as it headed north, coming to grief in a floating peat bog at Hareshaw Head near Bellingham in Northumberland.

What happened next is open to debate. The Form 1180 (Loss Card) for AG617 suggests that Flying Officer Fisher was still in the cockpit at the time of the crash, buried some sixteen feet underground. The view of his surviving family member, John's brother Frank, whom I interviewed at his home in Edinburgh, was that John's body was buried even deeper; two feet deeper, forward of the cockpit.

I find both claims difficult to believe for two reasons. First, because Flying Officer Fisher's body was recovered soon after the crash; second, because of the difficulty ACIA members had when we recovered part of AG617 some 63 years later with the considerable help of mechanical diggers. It is doubtful that the RAF maintenance team sent to recover Fisher's body and the wreckage of AG617 could have dug down so far without making a very large hole; yet we found that the deeper we dug, the more the sides collapsed in and the more dangerous and unstable the site became.

The Aftermath

The publicity generated by the ACIA recovery jogged a few local memories which I believe shed some light on the crash itself and the subsequent recovery of Flying Officer Fisher's body. Witnesses have stated that on the day of the crash an aircraft was heard overhead with its engine coughing and spluttering. Soon afterwards, a thud was heard in the distance. Also, and most importantly, a parachute was found at the crash site wrapped around the tail of the aircraft, with Flying Officer Fisher's body on or near the surface.

My conclusion as to the cause of the accident is that AG617 suffered engine problems; and that Flying Officer Fisher was aware of the problems but could not correct the situation and so attempted to bail out. Recovery of his flying helmet helped to confirm the fact that he had tried to escape, it being obvious that it had been pulled off when he attempted to exit the aircraft – but he was too low and simply ran out of time.

Frank Fisher maintains that, because the Mustang was not flying from its usual base of RAF Clifton but from RAF East Moor, a bomber airfield, and was thus not in the care of its own ground crew, there may not have been the same meticulous degree of servicing required by fighter aircraft, which could possibly account for the resultant engine trouble. However, this remains open to debate and is impossible to confirm.

The Crash Site

The recovery of AG617 was attempted on 2nd/3rd September 2006. The weather conditions were appalling, with continuous moderate to heavy rain throughout. This made it difficult to work, but since the machinery and access platforms were on site there could be no delay. An excavator and tractor were driven up from Sundaysight, the tractor carrying the heavy wooden supports we needed to take the weight of the excavator when it was on the boggy surface.

Once the excavator was on site and safely positioned, and the correct procedures had been undertaken with regard to crowd safety (there were about twenty people in attendance to view the recovery work), we began to take away the surface at the rate of about one foot per scrape. Pieces of twisted aluminium began to appear at a depth of about five feet; but the first real discovery was Flying Officer Fisher's flying helmet which confirmed beyond doubt the Mustang's identity. Most finds were at depths of between eight and twelve feet; these included the oil tank and engine bearer, a .50 calibre nose-mounted machine gun, parts of the nose section, the propeller and a lot of twisted metal.

The recovery lasted 4½ hours. Eventually it was decided, in conjunction with the operator of the excavator, that the size of the hole and the appalling weather conditions made the operation too hazardous to continue. At a depth of around twelve to fourteen feet the sides of the hole

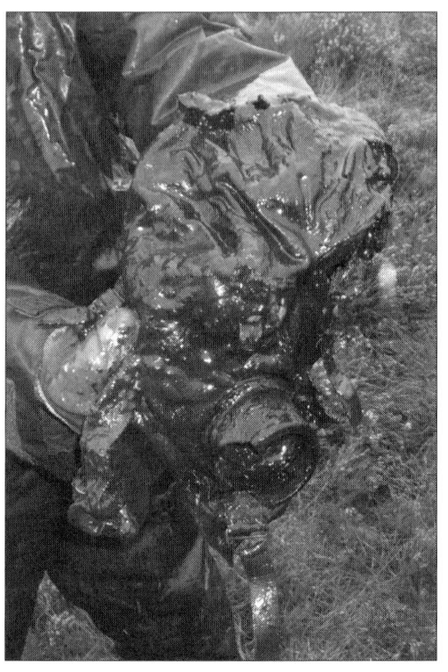

John Fisher's flying helmet.

The propeller is pulled out of the pit. (R. Gray)

***The main dig starts in earnest in 2006.* (R. Gray)**

and the surrounding ground were beginning to collapse in, and it was felt that the excavator had reached its maximum safe depth of operation. The recovery was halted in the knowledge that there was a lot more of the aircraft just out of reach.

The material recovered was removed to a barn and then taken on to the North East Aircraft Museum, where it is currently on display. Flying Officer Fisher's flying helmet was offered to his brother Frank, who kindly chose to let us keep and display it on his brother's behalf.

This was a tragic story not only because of the death of Flying Officer John Fisher, but also because of the death of John's other brother, George, on 6th July 1944 whilst flying a Hawker Typhoon of No 164 Squadron which crashed into the English Channel when returning from an operation over France. Unlike John, George's body was never found; his name is inscribed on a panel of the Runnymede Memorial in Surrey, which commemorates all those who lost their lives during the Second World War whilst serving with the Air Forces of the Commonwealth at bases in Great Britain or in north-western Europe, and who have no known grave.

Frank Fisher, last of the three brothers, was languishing at RAF Tempsford in Bedfordshire awaiting orders to train as aircrew when he heard of George's death. Because Frank was now the sole-surviving brother, all three of whom had joined the RAF, it was decided that he was not to undergo aircrew training. Perhaps it had been realised that the Fisher family had given enough.

Russell Gray

20

Piper PA28-181 Cherokee Archer II G-BHDG

Aircraft Type:	Piper PA-28-181 Cherokee Archer II
Registration:	G-BHDG
Operator:	Privately Owned
Crew:	Instructor Pilot: Mervyn Donnell Pilot under Supervision: Peter Hart
Passengers:	Jim Winning Findlay Guild
Crash Date:	13th February 1979
Crash Location:	Hedgehope Hill, six miles south-west of Wooler
Grid Reference:	80/939196

The Aircraft

The first prototype of the Piper PA-28 Cherokee, designed for pilot training and personal use, flew on 14th January 1960. The first production example flew just over a year later, on 10th February 1961, since when this all-metal four-seater has remained in production. During that time the basic design has been developed and modified to produce an impressive and varied range of models powered by numerous versions of the Avco Lycoming O-320 piston engine.

One of the early developments was the PA-28-180 Cherokee, introduced in 1962 and powered by the 180 hp O-320-A2A. This model was further developed and, in 1974, was renamed the Cherokee Challenger; new features included a modest increase in wingspan and fuselage length, better onboard equipment and an improved interior finish. In 1974 the Cherokee Challenger underwent another change of name, becoming the Cherokee Archer.

Crashed 13th February 1979

The Crash

At 07.36 hours on 13th February 1979, PA-28-181 Cherokee Archer II G-BHDG took off from Edinburgh Airport. The aircraft, built and delivered the previous year, was carrying four employees of H. G. Antipollution Ltd: Peter Hart and Findlay Guild were both joint directors of the firm, Jim Winning was a Sales Director, and Mervyn Donnell was a Salesman. The destination of the flight was Sunderland Airport (the four men were due to attend a business meeting at Birtley near Sunderland) and it was estimated that they would land there at around 08.45 hours. Instead they ended up lost amidst the blizzard-swept slopes of the Cheviot Hills, an area known locally as the 'graveyard of aeroplanes'.

Initially the flight went according to plan, with Peter Hart at the controls and Mervyn Donnell supervising him. Prior to take-off, Mervyn had telephoned for an update on the weather for the planned route, which took them south-east towards St Abbs Head VOR (VHF Omni-directional Range: a radio navigation beacon), situated on the coast to the north of Berwick-upon-Tweed. From there they were to fly south to Newcastle VOR and then continue their approach to Sunderland. The early stage of the flight was restricted to an altitude of 2,000 feet, but once outside the Edinburgh Airport control zone and having just passed St Abbs Head VOR they encountered a lowering cloud base, so Mervyn instructed Peter to begin a climb to 5,500 feet. On levelling off in cloud at the new altitude, the Cherokee's windscreen became obscured with ice and Mervyn drew Peter's attention to a build-up of ice on both wings.

Shortly afterwards there was a sudden vibration which Mervyn attributed to icing of the propeller, and so he suggested that they should descend. At this point Peter, with little experience of flying in such conditions, handed over the controls to Mervyn, who disconnected the autopilot

Cherokee G-BHDG seen on the hilltop once the blizzard had passed. **(P. Hart)**

***The wrecked cockpit as it appeared the following day.* (J. Corbett)**

and began a manual descent. By now the aircraft was being blown around quite severely by the prevailing winds, and the airspeed indicator started to fluctuate as the controls began to freeze. Mervyn had great difficulty in keeping the aircraft level, but to the relief of those inside, the ice began to break up and fall away as they descended through 3,500 feet and the airspeed indicator settled down.

Due to the strong winds encountered during the descent, Mervyn had lost track of their heading, so he attempted to obtain a cross-bearing from Talla VOR, located on the high ground to the north of Peebles. The aircraft was still flying in a thick snow cloud, so it was agreed that Mervyn should carry out a 180-degree turn in an effort to get them out of it. Unfortunately the winds had blown the aircraft six nautical miles west of their original track; they were now over the highest point of the Cheviot Hills.

As the aircraft continued to descend it struck a fence on a gently rising slope on the south-west summit of Hedgehope Hill, which rises to an altitude of 2,400 feet. Shortly after, it smashed into a snowdrift. The undercarriage legs and underside of the fuselage were torn away on the first impact and the engine nacelle and canopy were ripped open on the second, causing snow to blow into the now-exposed cockpit.

Mervyn was knocked unconscious on impact and Peter was seriously injured and in extreme pain; Jim and Findlay were relatively unscathed in the back of the cabin. Mervyn never regained consciousness and died from exposure 5½ hours after the crash. Peter, Jim and Findlay decided to stay with the aircraft in the hope that a rescue party would soon find them; but as midday approached and with the weather showing no signs of improvement, it was decided that both Jim and Findlay should set off for help.

As Peter scrambled into the rear luggage compartment to shelter from the blizzard, Jim and Findlay began their descent of the mountain. The going was slow due to the deep snowdrifts and biting winds but, some hours later, with their strength waning, the pair happened across the deserted farmhouse of Langleeford Hope in the valley below. Breaking in through a window, they found food and enough fuel to set a fire. Once dried out and with darkness falling, Jim and Findlay set off once again. This time the going was much easier and after a short time they stumbled across some fresh motorcycle tracks which led them to the lights of Langleeford Farm and the home of Walter Brown. It was now some ten hours after their aircraft had crashed.

Back at the crash site, Peter Hart prepared for the worst, knowing that with darkness falling and temperatures dropping rapidly the chances of him surviving the night were very slim. Fearing he would not be found in time, Peter wrote a goodbye note to his wife and one-year-old daughter, which he had not long finished when the Cherokee was illuminated by the searchlights of a search and rescue helicopter which had been scrambled from RAF Boulmer on the north-east coast immediately after the alarm had been raised. Peter was airlifted from the site nearly twelve hours after the crash, extremely lucky to have survived the ordeal. The body of Mervyn Donnell was recovered from the crash site the following morning; later it was established that he had died from his injuries and hypothermia.

***Peter Hart approaches Langleeford Hope on his return to the scene in 2008.* (Chris Davies)**

Peter Hart spent two months in Newcastle's Royal Victoria Infirmary and then a further two

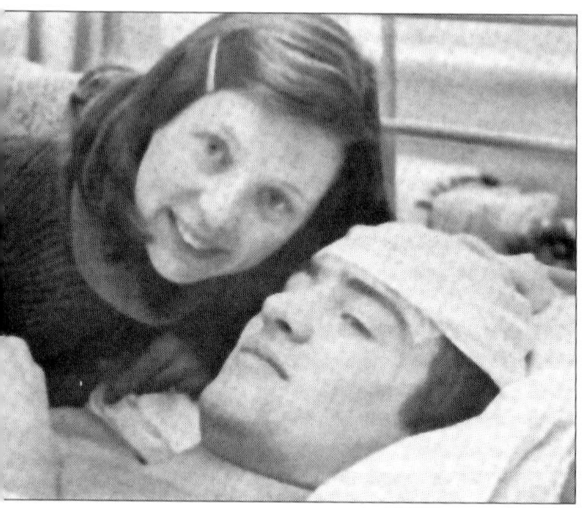

Peter Hart and his wife in Newcastle's Royal Infirmary after the crash. (P. Hart)

months at a hospital in Dunfermline. It was many months before he could walk again, but he went on to make a full recovery.

The Aftermath

The post-crash investigation concluded that there were no technical problems with the aircraft and that it was operating under power when it struck Hedgehope Hill. It would appear that it flew into the hill in zero visibility after the pilot became distracted due to the formation of ice on the aircraft, which resulted in him losing track of his heading. The strong winds evidently blew the aircraft some six nautical miles inland from its intended track, which placed the four men over dangerous terrain. Unaware of their true location, they unfortunately chose to descend over one of the highest points in Northumberland and the aircraft simply flew into the summit of Hedgehope Hill.

The Crash Site

At the site today there are no signs of the accident which took place during the winter of 1979. In the early 1990s all three main landing gears were present along with a scattering of smaller pieces but these now appear to have gone. However, the nose wheel and gear found its way into ACIA's collection via a third party in 2007.

Jim Corbett

Russell Gray and Peter Hart at the crash site in 2008. (Chris Davies)

21

Republic P-47D-21RE Thunderbolt 42-25530

Aircraft Type:	**Republic P47D-21RE Thunderbolt**
Serial:	42-25530
Code(s):	NOT KNOWN
Unit:	366th Fighter Squadron, 358th Fighter Group, 9th AF
Base:	RAF Millfield
Crew:	Pilot: 1st Lieutenant Anthony L. Serapiglia
Crash Date:	12th April 1944
Crash Location:	RAF Eshott, Northumberland
Grid Reference:	81/184974

The Aircraft

Along with the Hawker Typhoon, the Republic P-47 Thunderbolt was one of the largest and heaviest fighters produced during the Second World War, with a maximum loaded weight of 14,925 pounds. Ironically, the original requirement that lay behind the design and construction of the first two prototypes (the XP-47A and XP-47B) was for a lightweight fighter!

The P-47 was designed by Alexander Kartveli and submitted for approval to the US Army Air Force (USAAF) on 12th June 1940, and an order for a prototype followed on 6th September. The prototype XP-47B (40-3051) was powered by the colossal Pratt & Whitney R-2800 Double Wasp radial engine (Kartveli having decided to drop the lightweight fighter concept in favour of raw power and brute strength) and first took to the air on 6th May 1941 armed with eight .50 calibre machine guns In all respects this was a powerful aircraft with unparalleled destructive force for a single-engined fighter.

The first production model was the P-47B, which entered service

A P-47 Thunderbolt **(courtesy of the 303 Bomb Group Assoc.)**

powered by an even more powerful 2,000 hp R-2800-21 engine on 13th April 1942 with the 56th Fighter Group and the 78th Fighter Group, Eighth Air Force. Both units were among the many P-47 units that were deployed to Great Britain and Europe from January 1943 for use as long-range fighter escorts in conjunction with the P-51 Mustang. Early experience of such missions led to the addition of a 200-gallon drop tank beneath the fuselage; and the fuselage itself was lengthened to help improve manoeuvrability.

This model, the P-47D, was first ordered on 13th October 1941 and was by far the most successful member of the Thunderbolt family. Operational range was increased by the addition of wing pylons for two 150-gallon drop tanks; the engine was boosted to improve performance at high altitudes; and a fighter-bomber capability was introduced in the form of two 1,000 pound or three 500-pound bombs on the pylons and centreline station. Later production blocks introduced a 'bubble' canopy to greatly improve the pilot's all-round vision.

The P-47D was built by the thousands: 2,547 at Farmingdale on Long Island and 4,632 at Evansville, Indiana. Total P-47 production was 12,608. P-47D-21RE Thunderbolt 42-25530 was the fourth-from-last example built at Republic's Farmingdale site (the last was 42-25533) and was fairly new, with only 17 hours 50 minutes flying time, when it crashed. It was struck off the USAAF inventory in June 1944.

The Crash

There seem to be two accounts of the circumstances surrounding the crash; one American, the other British. What both versions agree on is that the mission involved four P-47 Thunderbolts operating from RAF Milfield as part of Course No 4 of the Fighter Leaders' Low Attack School; and that their mission was to practise strafing attacks on a motorised convoy moving south along the Felton to Morpeth road.

Colonel Glenn E. Duncan noted in his statement dated 12th April 1944 (the date of the accident) that the four aircraft split into two pairs and strafed individually at angles of 45 degrees to the column. His statement went on to say that as he approached an airfield he duly notified the other P-47 pilots by R/T. 'I had just finished an attack and noticed the two ships about two miles ahead of me turning to go down again. At this time they were in sight of the aerodrome but not inside the radius of traffic. A Spit, unseen by me until the collision, came from somewhere and met the P-47 somewhat head on.'

We are lucky enough to have another eyewitness account of the collision, but one that was taken on 17th April 1944, five days after the event. First Lieutenant John E. Hayden was flying as Colonel Duncan's wingman, so it is no surprise that his account of what happened was very similar to that provided by Colonel Duncan. However, he also stated that, after dive-bombing the convoy, the mission called for the P-47s to remain at low level and then strafe the convoy in pairs, criss-crossing their way to the back of the convoy.

After his attack, Lieutenant Serapiglia was about 200 yards behind his leader, flying at about 200 to 300 feet when, according to Hayden, 'a Spitfire suddenly appeared heading from east to west. Lieutenant Serapiglia's ship collided head-on with the Spitfire. The Spitfire went into a flat inverted spin

Two views of the crashed P-47D 42-25530. **(USAF)**

***The P-47's wing tip severed in the crash* (USAF).**

to the ground without burning. The P-47 lost a wing in the crash and, upon impact with the Spit, burst into flames and tumbled to the ground. The accident occurred at 11.45 about a mile and a half south of Eshott field.'

Neither of these statements apportions any blame to the Spitfire pilot, Sergeant Kai Knagenhjelm, nor to Lieutenant Serapiglia.

Bearing in mind that RAF Eshott was the base for No 57 OTU and therefore the majority of pilots operating from that base would have been novices, the RAF inquiry was understandably somewhat more damning. On the morning of the accident, Flying Officer Donald Higgin, the RAF instructor with 'C' Flight, authorised Sergeant Knagenhjelm to use Spitfire I R6762 to practise dogfighting skills with Lieutenant Hattren of the Royal Norwegian Air Force for 30 minutes, but not to fly below 5,000 feet. Once they had completed this exercise, both pilots were to climb to 8,000 feet and practise aerobatics, again for approximately 30 minutes.

Sergeant Knagenhjelm and Lieutenant Hattren took off at 10.25 hours to carry out their instructions. Lieutenant Hattren takes up the story. 'Having completed the exercise, I returned to base and was then told to remain in the air for a short time longer, as other aircraft were ready to land ahead of me. I also heard Sergeant Knagenhjelm calling on the R/T and knew he was in the circuit, and I saw him there. I heard him being given permission to land. I opened up and went on the outside of him. As I turned upwind I saw an explosion in the air at about 1,000 feet on my port side. I saw an aircraft spinning slowly doing about two or three turns before hitting the ground. This aircraft was on fire in the air. At the same time I saw another aircraft, also on fire, spinning horizontally until it finally dived into the ground and exploded.' Crucially, however, Lieutenant Hattren witnessed something else: several Thunderbolts and a Mustang flying a right-hand orbit of the airfield; a manoeuvre Lieutenant Hattren had some difficulty in avoiding.

Flying Officer Fernand Farfan, the instructor in 'B' Flight, also witnessed the accident, but this time from the ground whilst standing inside the perimeter track. Flying Officer Farfan's account essentially confirmed Lieutenant Hattren's version of events, but went on to explain what happened when the Thunderbolts appeared. 'I was watching aircraft in the circuit when I saw a Thunderbolt at about 600–700 feet, going in the opposite direction to the circuit and climbing fairly steeply. This aircraft passed a Spitfire on its starboard side. A second Thunderbolt, following the first one behind and to starboard, also climbed and the Spitfire appeared to fly through the port wing of the Thunderbolt.'

Five other eyewitnesses confirmed the same thing: the Thunderbolts were flying in the circuit but in the wrong direction, all but guaranteeing that there would be an accident. The miracle was that there was only one collision and not several.

The RAF investigation continued with a visit to RAF Milfield to take evidence from the Americans, but no witnesses could be found. The investigating officer, Wing Commander Eric Stammers, did manage to interview one of the pilots who had participated in the exercise, but who had not witnessed the collision. He claimed that Eshott was not on their maps and was so well camouflaged that they could not have known it was there. (As a result of the US Army Air Force's own investigation, we now know that Colonel Duncan *did* see the airfield.)

Wing Commander Stammers was unable to proceed any further with his investigation, having been informed by the adjutant that the American units were self-administering and independent, with no connection to the RAF.

As to the cause of the collision, I tend to agree with the RAF's assertion that the presence of the Thunderbolt flying into the circuit was down to bad briefing and bad navigation, and that the collision could not therefore be regarded as a 50:50 accident. Group Captain Bentley, the Officer Commanding RAF Eshott, went further and considered the blame fell squarely on the officer in charge of the American flight for 'leading his aircraft in such a manner as to cause considerable risk of collision in an airfield circuit' and 'the pilot of the Thunderbolt … for failing to keep an adequate lookout' when the weather was good and clear with visibility up to 20 miles. Group Captain Bentley went on to state that this was not an isolated incident; there had been several previous occasions when Thunderbolts had flown through the aerodrome circuit at low altitude.

The Crash Site

Most of the P-47 was recovered very soon after the accident, there having been enough manpower at RAF Milfield to enable the removal of the aircraft which was in close proximity to the airfield. It helped that the aircraft crashed in an easily accessible spot, effectively in the orbit of the airfield. Perhaps also it was thought that the sight of wreckage scattered over the ground on their final approach was not the most appropriate signal to send to trainee pilots! However, even today it is readily apparent that there was a crash in the field and the ground yields numerous poignant reminders without much effort. In February 2008 my colleague Chris Davies and I scanned the area with a metal detector (having first been given permission to do so by the landowner) and found engine casing, alloy pipework, fragments of skinning and even the tip of a .50 calibre machine gun bullet, the standard armament of the P-47. Perhaps deeper there may be more!

Russell Gray

The crash site as it looks today. **(R. Gray)**
(Inset) Parts of what are believed to the engine casing recovered from the site. **(R. Gray)**

22

Short Stirling III EH880

Aircraft Type:	**Short Stirling III**
Serial:	EH880
Code(s):	AA–J
Unit:	No 75 Squadron, RAF
Base:	RAF Mepal, Cambridgeshire
Crew:	Pilot: Warrant Officer George J. S. Kerr Navigator: Sergeant L. G. Copsey Wireless Operator: Sergeant D. F. Wort Engineer: Sergeant R. Smith Bomb Aimer: Flight Sergeant D. A. Holt Air Gunner: Sergeant K. Hook Air Gunner: Sergeant G. W. T. Lucas
Civilians:	Sylvia Robson, Ethel Robson, Margery Robson, William Robson, Sheila Robson
Crash Date:	1st December 1943
Crash Location:	Cliff House Farm, North Togston, Northumberland
Grid Reference:	81/249029

The Aircraft

When one thinks of the four-engined bombers used by the RAF during the Second World War, more often than not it is the Avro Lancaster that springs to mind; but the Lancaster did not commence operations until 1942. In the early years of the war, bombing raids were carried out by twin-engined aircraft such as the Armstrong Whitworth Whitley (see Chapter 1), Bristol Blenheim, Handley Page Hampden (see Chapter 11) and Vickers

Wellington (see Chapter 29). However, as the bombing campaign grew in importance, the Air Ministry called for larger aircraft able to carry heavier bomb loads over greater distances.

Short Brothers of Rochester in Kent responded with what would be the RAF's first four-engined monoplane bomber and the first to be used in the Second World War: the Short Stirling. Designed to Air Ministry Specification B12/36, it was able to carry 14,000 pounds of bombs over a distance of 740 miles (or 3,500 pounds over 2,010 miles), thus bringing many more targets in mainland Europe within range.

The Stirling prototype (L7600) first flew on 14th May 1939 but was promptly destroyed when it crashed on landing. A second prototype (L7605) took its place in the flight-test programme after it flew on 3rd December 1939. Five months later, on 7th May 1940, the first production Stirling I (N3635) undertook its maiden flight. Such was the need for Stirlings, 712 of which were ordered, that the Rochester line was complemented by production lines established in Belfast (Short & Harland) and Birmingham (Austin Motor Company) under sub-contract. Production was subsequently delayed because of German bombing of the Rochester and Belfast factories, but also because of technical problems with the aircraft itself.

The Stirling I entered operational service in August 1940 when the first examples were delivered to No 7 Squadron at RAF Leeming in Yorkshire; but it was not until the night of 10th/11th February 1941 that they undertook their first mission: an attack by three of the new bombers on oil facilities in Rotterdam.

In all, eight Bomber Command squadrons received the Stirling I; the only RAF heavy bomber to operate regularly by day and night during 1941. Defensive armament was considered to be good: eight .303 calibre machine guns in a nose turret (two), a mid-upper dorsal turret (two) and a tail turret (four). Early Stirling Is sported another pair of .303s in a remote-controlled ventral turret aft of the bomb bay.

A new type of dorsal turret and more powerful Bristol Hercules XVI engines were introduced on the next production model, the Stirling III, which entered service with No 15 Squadron at RAF Bourn in Cambridgeshire in late-1942; the first of fifteen squadrons to receive the Mk III. The new model's first operation was the bombing of Cologne on 14th February 1943. A total of 1,047 Stirling IIIs rolled off the three production lines and they continued to carry out bombing missions until 8th September 1944, when No 149 Squadron at RAF Methwold in Suffolk carried out the last Stirling raid of the war in which its aircraft bombed Le Havre.

During all this time the Stirling suffered from a major design shortcoming, the origins of which lay in Specification B12/36 itself. When first conceived by the Air Ministry, the Specification stipulated that the new bomber had to have a wingspan of less than 100 feet in order to fit into existing RAF hangars. Because the Stirling's fuselage measured over 87 feet in length, for reasons of aerodynamics the original wingspan was over 100 feet – too wide for the hangars. The wing span was duly cut back to an inch over 99 feet; but this adversely affected the amount of lift generated by the wing, which in turn increased the length of the Stirling's take-off run. In an attempt to solve the problem an extra-long main undercarriage unit was added to increase the aircraft's angle of attack and thus generate more lift.

The length of the undercarriage unit meant that the cockpit was some 22 feet above the runway. It also meant that a two-part structure was required so the undercarriage unit could bend and be retracted during flight. The weakness inherent in a long leg split into two sections to enable it to bend resulted in the Stirling's undercarriage being vulnerable to collapse.

***The Short Stirling was the first of the four-engine bombers to serve with Bomber Command.* (J. Shipley)**

In the air the undercarriage units, when retracted, left the large main wheels partly exposed, which increased drag. Combined with the inevitable increases in all-up weight as the Stirling was developed, the result was a painfully low maximum altitude of just 13,000 feet (there are reports of unloaded aircraft reaching 20,000 feet), making the Stirling an easy target for enemy flak batteries. It also left the Stirlings and their crews at risk from bombs dropped by the higher-flying Halifaxes and Lancasters.

It is said that Lancaster and Halifax crews would cheer when they heard that Stirlings were to take part on the same bombing operations – they knew that the Stirlings, flying at lower altitudes, would be on the receiving end of most of the flak and fighter gunfire. Nevertheless, the Stirling was very popular with the aircrews that flew in her; and the shorter wing had one plus point in that the reduction in span increased the bomber's manoeuvrability, allowing it to make very tight turns – a very useful trait when attacked by fighters.

Stirling III EH880 was one of a batch produced by the Austin Motor Company at its Longbridge factory in Birmingham, to Contract No B. 982939/39, and was initially delivered to No 75 (New Zealand) Squadron on 17th May 1943. The squadron had been operational with the type from November 1942 when Stirlings replaced the Wellingtons it had been flying since April 1940. It would appear from the Form 78 (Movement Card) that EH880 suffered some damage in June 1943; however it was returned to the squadron on 24th July, and on 30th July took part in the large Bomber Command raid on Hamburg. It continued to participate in bombing raids, including a large-scale attack on the Peenemünde V2 rocket-testing site on the Baltic coast on the night of 17th/18th August; and on 18th/19th November it was one of 18 aircraft put up by the squadron to attack Mannheim – the last Bomber Command raid of the Second World War to involve over 100 Stirlings.

The Crash

At approximately 15.16 hours on 1st December 1943, Stirling III EH880 of No 75 Squadron took off from RAF Mepal in Cambridgeshire with a payload of sea mines destined for the cold waters around Denmark. The squadron had been briefed to carry out 'Gardening' operations: laying mines in coastal waters to hamper the German Navy and the merchant ships that supplied the country. These operations were fairly frequent, with various target areas being given plant-like names; on this occasion 19 Stirlings and 12 Halifaxes had been detailed to 'sow' their mines off Denmark and the Frisian Islands.

Whilst returning from the operation, EH880 was diverted to RAF Acklington in Northumberland due to fog, and at 22.00 hours the aircraft approached the airfield from the north-east to land. Unfortunately the pilot had become slightly lost in the fog, and misjudged his location, assuming that he was closer to RAF Acklington than he actually was. As he reduced his altitude prior to landing, he must have had no idea that he was actually still some 1½ miles north-east of the airfield. Moments later the Stirling collided with the upper floor of Cliff House Farm, North Togston, home to the Robson family.

Within a split-second the family home had been reduced to burning rubble, with most of the top floor destroyed. More tragic still was the fact that the five Robson children – Sylvia (aged 9), Ethel (7), Margery (5), William (3) and Sheila (19 months) – were all asleep in the upstairs bedrooms while their parents, William and Norah Robson, played cards downstairs with friends Jim and Evelyn Rowell. As William and Norah struggled from the rubble that once had been their house, they noticed that one man had struggled from the wreckage that had been Stirling III EH880, and was on fire. Jim Rowell promptly dragged the rear gunner, Sergeant Hook, to safety and rolled him on the ground to put

The Robson children, taken not long before the fateful day when the Stirling hit their house and they were all killed. **(Mrs Young, via D. Walton)**

Small remains of Stirling EH880 found in the plough soil. Although it is not possible to identify which part of the aircraft that the aluminium and Perspex came from, the piece of wood appears to be part of one of the propellers. **(J. Shipley)**

out the flames. Tragically, the six other members of EH880's crew, along with all five of the Robsons' children, died instantly when the aircraft hit Cliff House Farm.

The Aftermath

This terrible accident shocked the people who lived in and around the Togston and Amble area. In the weeks that followed the crash the wreckage was cleared, and the remains of the crew were laid to rest in cemeteries in their local areas; apart from the pilot, Warrant Officer George Kerr, who was buried in nearby Chevington Cemetery, where he lies today with many other airmen who lost their lives during the Second World War. The Robson children, who had been well-known in the area as they had helped their father on his milk round, were all laid to rest in Amble West Cemetery.

Cliff House Farm was rebuilt, but William and Norah Robson never returned to it. Having moved out of the area to Fenrother, they tried for another child a year later, but it was stillborn. When William died in 1982, and Norah passed away in 1988, their bodies were brought to Amble and laid to rest along with their children.

The Crash Site

Up until the 1980s Togston Bank Farm occupied the site that was once Cliff House Farm, but in the late 1980s it was demolished. Now the site that was once the scene of such tragedy is, like so many other similar sites, a ploughed field, the only evidence that an aircraft once crashed there being the small fragments of aluminium and Perspex that sometimes appear after harvest. However, the people of the area never forgot the tragedy, and a few years ago a new housing estate built on the road between Togston and Amble, a short distance away from the crash site, was named Cliff House Farm Estate. The main road on the estate is named Robson's Way. This in turn leads to Sheila's Close, Sylvia's Close, William's Close, Ethel's Close, and Marjorie's Close: an unusual memorial to the five children who died so tragically on the night of 1st December 1943.

Jonathan Shipley

The grave of the five Robson children who were killed when EH880 crashed into the upper floor of Cliff House Farm. **(Author)**

23

Supermarine Spitfire IAs R6596 and X4595

Aircraft Type:	**Supermarine Spitfire Mk IA**
Serials:	R6596 and X4595
Codes:	NOT KNOWN
Unit:	No 57 Operational Training Unit, RAF
Base:	RAF Eshott, Northumberland
Crew:	Pilot (R6596): Pilot Officer James M. Flood Pilot (X4595): Flight Sergeant William A. Lynn
Crash Date:	17th March 1944
Crash Location:	Hepburn Moor, Northumberland
Grid Reference:	NOT KNOWN

The Aircraft

Think about the RAF during the Second World War, and more often than not the first image that comes to mind is that of the crucial and defining role played by RAF Fighter Command in the Battle of Britain; and synonymous with that part of the conflict is the sight and sound of the one aircraft that all readers of this book will have heard of and be familiar with: the Supermarine Spitfire.

When the Air Ministry issued Specification F7/30 for a single-seat day/night-fighter armed with four .303 calibre machine guns to replace the RAF's Bristol Bulldog biplane fighters, Supermarine Aviation's chief designer, Reginald Mitchell, responded with the Type 224. This was Mitchell's first fighter design and was a somewhat ungainly aircraft notable for its inverted gull wing and heavily trousered undercarriage.

The Type 224 flew in February 1934, but it proved to be a disappointment. However, when the Air Ministry issued Specifications F5/34 and F10/35 for a single-engined, single-seat day/night-fighter armed with eight .303s, the primary purpose of which was to intercept and destroy enemy bombers, Mitchell and his team drew on the experience gained with the Type 224 and their tremendous success in designing and developing Schneider Trophy-winning high-speed seaplanes to produce what at first was known as the Type 300, but which later was christened Spitfire after the name was suggested by Sir Robert MacLean, the managing director of Vickers Armstrong.

The Spitfire prototype (K5054) flew for the first time on 5th March 1936 with ex-Flying Officer Joseph 'Mutt' Summers (chief test pilot) at the controls. A legend had been born. Successful flight-testing over the coming months led to an initial order in June 1936 for 310 Spitfire Is, the first of which (K9798) joined No 19 Squadron at RAF Duxford in Cambridgeshire on 4th August 1938.

When war was declared on 3rd September 1939, nine squadrons in RAF Fighter Command were operational with Spitfire Is and another two were in the process of re-equipping. On 16th October a Spitfire I of No 603 (City of Glasgow) Squadron downed a Heinkel He 111 bomber over the Firth of Forth (another was despatched a few minutes later by No 602 (City of Edinburgh) Squadron), these being the first German aircraft to be shot down over Great Britain since 1918.

The original Spitfire Mk Is were armed with four .303 calibre machine guns, but combat experience led to the Mk IA with eight .303s and then the Mk IB with four .303s and four 20mm cannons. A total of 1,567 were built, and they equipped no less than nineteen squadrons at the start of the Battle of Britain in May 1940.

Spitfire IA X4595 was a 'presentation' aircraft called *Tamilnad*. A total of £22,500 had been raised by the *Madras Mail* Spitfire fund to build the aircraft and thus help with the war effort. Many aircraft funded by subscription flew during the war, often taking the names of cities or regions where the money to build them was raised. The name of this particular aircraft came from a region in south-east India in which Tamil is the dominant language. It had previously served with No 72 Squadron in the Battle of Britain (during which it claimed a 'damaged' Messerschmitt Bf 110) before being transferred to No 57 Operational Training Unit (OTU) at RAF Eshott in Northumberland.

The Crash

At 09.05 hours on 17th March 1944, a group of aspiring RAF pilots took off from RAF Eshott for a training flight. Flying Spitfire IA X4595 was Sergeant William Lynn, who had been officially promoted that day to Flight Sergeant but was unaware of this at the time of the flight. Another of the pilots was Canadian Pilot Officer James Flood in Spitfire IA R6596. Both aircraft were survivors of the Battle of Britain.

William Lynn was born on 29th May 1923 in Jarrahmond, just five miles west of the timber town of Orbost in Australia. He was one of many Australians who answered the call to fight during the Second World War, and he enlisted in the Royal Australian Air Force on 26th June 1942 at the age of nineteen. After his initial training in Australia, Leading Aircraftman Lynn embarked for Canada on 30th April 1943 for the next stage of training to be a fighter pilot. Here he earned his pilot's badge on 17th September 1943, which made him an Airman Pilot. From here he was posted to No 1 Operational Training Unit (OTU) at Bagotville until he departed for Great Britain on 26th December 1943.

Sergeant William Lynn arrived in Great Britain on 11th January 1944 and reported to RAF Eshott on 29th February. The base was home to No 57 OTU and trained future Spitfire pilots.

Spitfire X4595. **(N. Anderson)**

Thirty-five minutes into the flight on 17th March, during practice in the difficult art of formation flying, Lynn and Flood collided whilst commencing a turn. Flood's Spitfire struck Lynn's Spitfire from below and behind at approximately 2,000 feet, taking its tail off with the propeller and leaving no possible chance for Lynn to recover his aircraft or to bail out.

The Aftermath

According to the Form 1180 (Loss Card), Pilot Officer Flood struggled to maintain control of his aircraft and 'span down and regained control for further landing'. This belly-landing, which Flood survived, happened at Birchwood Hall. He was not blamed for the collision – the loss of life at all of the north-east OTUs was well known during the war and a real risk every time pilots took to the sky – and lessons were learnt from this tragic accident.

Later in the war, Flying Officer James Flood was assigned to No 421 (Red Indian) Squadron, Royal Canadian Air Force, and on 28th August 1944 flew an armed reconnaissance mission over the Dieppe area of France. During the mission his aircraft was engaged in a fatal encounter with an FW 190. He is buried at Dieppe Canadian War Cemetery in Hautot-sur-mer, France.

The grave of Flight Sergeant Lynn.
(Courtesy of Dave Young)

The Crash Site

Members of ACIA put a great deal of effort into finding any living relatives to whom we may be able to pass on information about their loved ones. In July 2007 we were joined in Northumberland by David Young and Paula Stevens, relatives of Flight Sergeant Lynn. David, who had flown in from Australia, and Paula, who was already working in Great Britain, travelled to Northumberland to visit the general crash area and help with the search of the moor.

Even with help from local farmer Daniel Spoors, his father Lawrence and local shepherd Gordon Rogerson, we have not yet been able to pinpoint the exact location of this crash, despite a number of searches. It is believed that this site may have been excavated in the past. When we do find it and have some evidence, David and Paula will be the first to know.

Neil Anderson

24

Supermarine Spitfire IIA P8528

Aircraft Type:	**Supermarine Spitfire IIA**
Serial:	P8528
Code(s):	NOT KNOWN
Unit:	No 57 Operational Training Unit, RAF
Base:	RAF Eshott, Northumberland
Crew:	Pilot: Pilot Officer M. B. L. J. M. C. Neve de Mervegnies
Crash Date:	9th April 1943
Crash Location:	Weldon Bridge, Northumberland
Grid Reference:	81/125988

The Aircraft

By June 1940, the Spitfire II had been developed with the more powerful 1,175 hp Rolls-Royce Merlin XII engine, giving a top speed of 357 mph (22 mph faster than the Merlin II/III-powered Mk Is). Again, differences in the armament configuration identified two variants: the Mk IIA (eight .303 calibre machine guns) and the Mk IIB (four .303s and two 20mm cannons). Production at the Castle Bromwich Aircraft Factory in Birmingham ran to 920 examples (75 As and 170 Bs), some of which were later converted to Mk V.

The first Spitfire IIAs entered service in July 1940 and their first operational sortie was with No 611 (West Lancashire) Squadron based at RAF Duxford on 31st August 1940. The squadron developed its role, flying the first 'Rhubarb' daylight fighter sweeps over France.

Spitfire IIA P8528 was initially delivered to No 5 Maintenance Unit at RAF Kemble in Gloucestershire on 26th May 1941. A 'presentation' aircraft, it was named *Township of Shipley* after the town of Shipley in West

Spitfire P8528 **Township of Shipley** *seen here while serving with 315 (Deblin) Squadron about two years prior to crashing at Weldon Bridge.* **(Alfred Price)**

Yorkshire, which had donated £6,472 from fund-raising events. Just over two weeks later, on 11th June, P8528 was delivered to the Polish Wing based at RAF Northolt in Middlesex, from where it was assigned to No 308 (Krakow) Squadron on 26th June for operational duties with the codes ZF–I.

After only one month with the unit, P8528 was transferred to No 315 (Deblin) Squadron and recoded PK–J, with the lady's name Janka added to the J. A month later the aircraft was transferred to the Rolls-Royce factory at Hucknall in Nottinghamshire. This brief stay lasted about six weeks before, on 8th October, P8528 was assigned to No 130 (Punjab) Squadron at RAF Portreath in Cornwall for convoy patrol duties.

Another change of ownership came on 23rd October when P8528 was taken on charge by No 133 (Eagle) Squadron based at RAF Eglinton in Northern Ireland (now Derry Airport), but the aircraft overturned on landing after the ferry flight. The resulting damage meant that P8528 did not join No 133 Squadron until 10th December.

A few weeks later it moved once again, when it was taken on charge by No 134 Squadron who also operated from Eglinton. It was with No 134 Squadron that P8528 spent most of its operational life, carrying out convoy patrols; however the aircraft's Form 78 (Movement Card) states that it was temporarily transferred to No 53 Operational Training Unit (OTU) during March 1942 for a two-week period. The reason for this short-term transfer is unclear, but on 31st December 1942 it changed units for the final time when it was taken on charge by No 57 OTU.

No 57 OTU was formed at RAF Hawarden in Clwyd, Wales, in November

1940 to train single-seat fighter pilots after they had passed their basic pilot training. In late 1942 the unit moved to the 'almost finished' RAF Eshott in Northumberland, and commenced training with Miles Masters, Fairey Battles and Supermarine Spitfires. It was quite common for the Spitfires in use to have served with operational front-line squadrons, so the fact that P8528 had served with five other units and had a 'history' was not at all unusual.

The Crash

On the morning of 9th April 1943, Spitfire IIA P8528 took off from RAF Eshott on a training flight. In the cockpit was Pilot Officer Michael Neve de Mervegnies, a young Belgian from Ougrée. Born on 3rd June 1923, Neve de Mevergnies was at high school when war broke out, and embarked for England from Calais on 25th May 1940 as German forces swept through the Low Countries and France.

On 6th September 1940 he volunteered for the Belgian forces in Great Britain, and on 7th August 1941 he joined the RAF. Basic pilot training commenced on 20th December with No 6 Elementary Flying Training School (EFTS) at RAF Sywell in Northamptonshire, followed by a period with No 10 EFTS at RAF Filton in Gloucestershire from 4th April 1942, prior to a move to No 22 Service Flight Training School at RAF Calveley in Cheshire on 19th August 1942.

Once his basic training was complete, Neve de Mevergnies moved to No 57 OTU on 2nd March 1943 and was commissioned, becoming a Pilot Officer. This was his last training post prior to moving to an operational squadron – but he was destined never to make it to a front-line unit.

P/O Neve de Mervegnies, who lost his life when Spitfire P8528 crashed. **(via A. Bar)**

Crashed 9th April 1943

About 45 minutes after taking off, P8528 crashed near Weldon Bridge, north of Morpeth. During his dawn flight Neve de Mevergnies had been granted permission to carry out low flying, but he was not permitted to fly below 300 feet. As he approached the River Coquet, and the small settlement of Weldon Bridge near the Great North Road (now the A1), Neve de Mevergnies chose to drop down to a height of just 75 feet in an attempt to fly under high-tension cables. Unfortunately he hit the lower cables, and the collision caused P8528 to crash into trees on the edge of the B6344 near Togstead Farm.

The crash caused the Spitfire to break up, scattering wreckage throughout the thin tree line and into the fields adjacent to the river. Pilot Officer Neve de Mevergnies died instantly. Thus, at the age of just nineteen, another foreign airman had lost his life on British soil and would not live to see his country free again. Given that he was only a matter of days away from joining an operational unit, it seems all the more tragic that a brave young man should meet such an untimely death. However, his story was, unfortunately, all too common during the war years.

The Aftermath

On 15th April 1943 Pilot Officer Neve de Mevergnies' body was laid to rest at Brookwood Cemetery. Just over four years later, on 29th October 1949, he was re-interred at Cointe Sclessin in his homeland. One of Belgium's young sons had finally returned home.

The Crash Site

Although no wreckage of Spitfire P8528 remains at the location where it crashed, today the point at which the aircraft came to rest against the tree line can still be seen. This positive identification is largely thanks to a photograph taken at the time by a man serving with No 57 OTU who visited the site. In the photo the trees and fence are visible, and although they have obviously grown, the same trees can still be seen along with the fence. The field across which the aircraft skidded is now used, as it was then, for grazing, while the high-tension cables that Neve de Mervegnies tried to fly under still cross the landscape to the west.

Jonathan Shipley

25

Supermarine Spitfire VA P8563

Aircraft Type:	Supermarine Spitfire IIA (converted to VA)
Serial:	P8563
Code(s):	FL–J
Unit:	No 81 Squadron, RAF
Base:	RAF Eshott, Northumberland
Crew:	Pilot: Pilot Officer Harold J. Appel
Crash Date:	27th March 1942
Crash Location:	Dead Friars, four miles north of Stanhope
Grid Reference:	Crash site still to be located

The Aircraft

The Supermarine Spitfire, the darling of the Battle of Britain, has become a legend in its own lifetime; not just within the RAF fraternity but throughout the world. However, while most people think of it as a day-fighter tasked with intercepting and downing German bombers heading for targets in Great Britain, the versatility of the basic design also led to its use as a highly effective fighter-bomber that operated at home and overseas.

The Spitfire Mk VA was fitted with the more powerful 1,445 hp Merlin 45 engine which gave a maximum speed of 374 mph, and was armed with eight .303 calibre machine guns. In addition, a centreline rack could carry one 500-pound bomb or an auxiliary fuel tank.

Production of the Mk V family ran to 6,487 examples, of which 2,482 were Mk VCs. Some Mk Vs were originally laid down as Mk IIs but completed as Mk Vs; others were Mk IIs upgraded to Mk V standard later in their career. One of the latter conversions was P8563, which was a 'presentation' Spitfire, having been paid for with funds raised through the Lord Mayor of

Crashed 27th March 1942

Leicester's Spitfire Fund, hence its name *City of Leicester 1*.

Fund-raising for the purpose of raising money for weapons of war has a long tradition in our history and was wholeheartedly encouraged by the Churchill government. Lord Beaverbrook, the Minister for Aircraft Production, suggested a price of £5,000 for a Spitfire airframe – a figure substantially short of the genuine cost of approximately £12,000. The lucky individual, organisation, town or city would have their name stencilled on the side of the Spitfire in four-inch-high yellow letters.

According to the Form 78 (Movement Card), P8563 was manufactured at Castle Bromwich as a Spitfire Mk II and taken on charge by No 5 Maintenance Unit at RAF Kemble in Gloucestershire on 26th May 1941. On 14th July 1941 the aircraft was allotted to No 315 (Deblin) Squadron at RAF Northolt in Middlesex but immediately transferred to No 308 (Danzig) Squadron on the same day. Both squadrons formed part of the RAF's Polish Wing.

It is unclear exactly when P8563 returned to No 315 Squadron, but it was with this unit that the aircraft had its first success on 29th August 1941. Flown by Sergeant Aleksander Chudek, P8563 claimed two Messerschmitt Bf 109Es near Lumbers and St Omer whilst flying a 'Circus' sortie (operations by small numbers of bombers escorted by very large numbers of fighters, designed primarily to bring enemy fighters up to fight). At this time the aircraft was coded PK–E; however, Phil Smith's research has indicated that, unusually, two aircraft with No 315 Squadron could have been coded 'E', which would cause some

Spitfire P8563 City of Leicester. (R. Nixon)

confusion as to the actual number of 'kills' attributed to P8563. (Sadly, Warrant Officer Aleksander Chudek, DFM, VM, CV was killed in action over the English Channel on 23rd June 1944 in Spitfire AB271 with No 302 (Poznan) Squadron. His body was never recovered. It is very likely that his flying log book would provide the answer to this puzzle.)

On 6th September 1941, P8563 was returned to Air Service Training Ltd at RAF Hamble in Hampshire for repair and to be converted to Mk VA configuration. The aircraft was then sent via No 39 Maintenance Unit to No 81 Squadron based at RAF Ouston in Northumberland, with whom it was to carry the codes FL–J.

The Crash

On 27th March 1942 Pilot Officer Harold Appel took off from RAF Ouston in Spitfire VA P8563 as 'Blue 2' to Flight Sergeant P. J. Anson for an operational patrol over the coast around Seaham Harbour in County Durham. Born in Tavistock, Canada, Appel was the youngest son of Andrew and Alma Appel. In July 1940 he enlisted in the Royal Canadian Air Force (RCAF) and, following his training in the British Commonwealth Air Training Plan, he received his wings on 20th August 1941. In September Pilot Officer Appel proceeded to England for more training before being transferred to No 81 Squadron in December 1941.

The weather was terrible when the two Spitfires took off: cloud at 10/10 from 700–1,000 feet and 10/10 at ground level over the hills. To make matters worse, Pilot Officer Appel seemed not to be in radio contact with base. The Court of Inquiry maintained that he 'was neither in transmission or reception with the ground otherwise he would have broken cloud further north … as it was the aircraft

P/O Harold J. Appel.
(J. Smith)

was pointing in a south-westerly direction'. The Operational Records Book for No 81 Squadron states that the cloud base was very low and that the section was vectored 'too far west over high ground'. Pilot Officer Appel then lost sight of his section leader and flew into high ground. As if to reinforce this view, it was stated in the Court of Inquiry that Appel made no attempt to vacate the aircraft by parachute, and that there was no reason to believe the Spitfire had suffered any structural failure.

The Aftermath

The reason for the accident seems fairly straightforward: Pilot Officer Appel, considered to be a very able pilot who finished fifth in his class, but who was relatively inexperienced in instrument flying when he found himself lost in cloud, dropped lower to try to find his bearings whilst unaware that he was over the hills, and simply flew into the ground. At the time of his death he had accumulated some 37¼ hours on Hurricanes and 31 hours on Spitfires, and an overall total of 141 hours solo on all types.

The Crash Site

Phil Smith has spent many hours tracing surviving eyewitnesses and trawling through RAF paperwork in order to discover the crash site of P8563, but when it comes down to it you need a large amount of luck. Several visits were made to the broad location of the crash and many hours were spent searching. We studied the written evidence, possible directions of flight, all the hills and valleys in the perceived path of flight and any eyewitness reports we could find. Attempts were also made to locate any surviving eyewitnesses and to try to persuade them to go down to the crash site. Finally, however, my metal detector found something that was more than barbed wire and fence posts, and in a little depression in the ground we found a small bulb. This was obviously not part of any tractor or farm machine, and further examination of tho area yielded more and more aircraft parts. We had found an aircraft crash site, but was it that of P8563? We would not know the answer to that question until our next visit.

According to Ministry of Defence rules and regulations, certain conditions have to be met to obtain a licence even to dig on a crash site, the first being the positive identification of the aircraft concerned. To do

The archaeologist maps out the crash site. (R. Gray)

this we might have to look for, say, an engine plate; but in the case of P8563 we were incredibly lucky: on our second visit we found the wing machine gun cover with the serial 'P8563' handwritten on the inside. However, this amazing find had to be left with all the other finds on site, since all we had was the permission of the landowner to search but not to recover any artefacts; and certainly not to dig for anything.

Now we had to fulfil all the criteria required for a recovery to take place: the permission of the landowners; the sure and certain identification of the aircraft (which we had done); and finally, an assurance that the pilot's remains had been recovered from the site and buried in the correct fashion. Satisfying this last requirement was not difficult as we had Pilot Officer Appel's death certificate and burial location.

It is worth mentioning that one more condition must be met that mainly applies to bombers, namely that there is no ordnance associated with the aircraft. In general, bombers that crashed on return from a mission, for example Hampden I L4054 (see Chapter 11), would be deemed by the Ministry of Defence to be unsuitable for recovery; but bombers that crashed on training flights, for example Wellington IC X3171 (see Chapter 29), would be looked upon more favourably.

Finally, the Ministry of Defence issued the recovery licence and Phil Smith set the date for recovery at 9th March 2008. Due to the area being designated an Area of Special Scientific Interest the dig had to be done by hand. An area was allocated for the spoil and, as we cut away the top surface, we began to find parts of the Spitfire: cockpit switches and instruments were pulled out of the mud. A shift pattern was organised with two or three diggers in the hole and several helpers removing the wet mud in buckets.

Radio fuze dated 1940, recovered from the site. **(R. Allenby)**

Other finds included an oxygen regulator. **(R. Allenby)**

After several hours the archaeologist halted the work in order to record the area accurately and study, photograph and record all the finds before placing them into plastic bags for future examination. Once we had dug down to our maximum depth of 1.6 metres and all the interesting artefacts had been removed, the hole was filled in, the area cleaned up and as far as possible returned to how we found it. Alas, the dig had not answered any of the questions as to why the Spitfire had crashed. The only person who knew the real answer was Pilot Officer Appel.

Russell Gray

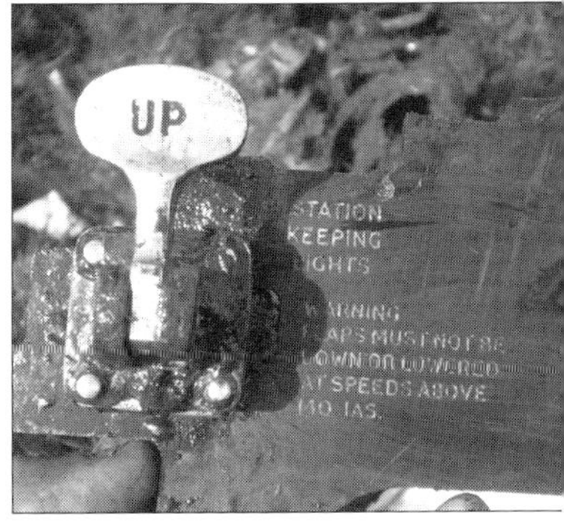

The cockpit flaps control switch. **(R.Allenby)**

26

Supermarine Spitfire VB AA920

Aircraft Type:	**Supermarine Spitfire VB (clipped wing)**
Serial:	AA920
Code(s):	NOT KNOWN
Unit:	No 57 Operational Training Unit, RAF
Base:	RAF Eshott, Northumberland
Crew:	Pilot: Flight Sergeant Edwin K. Pannett (RAFVR)
Crash Date:	18th April 1945
Crash Location:	North-west of Longhorsley, Northumberland
Grid Reference:	81/139959

The Aircraft

The Supermarine Spitfire VB was perhaps the best-known variant of the type. The Mk V was first delivered to squadrons in February 1941 and was powered by the 1,440 hp Merlin 45 engine. The VB was armed with four .303 calibre machine guns and two 20mm cannons, which in 1941 gave it very destructive firepower and the ability to take on any of the modern German fighters.

For its role as a fighter-bomber the Mk VB could carry one 500-pound bomb on a centreline rack, which could also be used to carry an auxiliary fuel drop tank to boost operational range. The Mk VB was also the first of the family to be widely used overseas when fifteen aircraft were delivered to Malta (by aircraft carrier) on 7th March 1942.

Spitfire VB AA920 was built by Vickers Armstrong Ltd at Southampton under Contract No B. 19713/39 and was certified fit for service with the RAF on 18th November 1941. It was first delivered to No 33 Maintenance Unit, then to No 72 Squadron at RAF Gravesend in Kent on 30th November

Crashed 18th April 1945

A Supermarine Spitfire VB. **(North East Aircraft Museum)**

1941. Unfortunately it suffered a flying accident on 2nd March 1942, but the damage was not serious and after repair it returned to the squadron. On 24th March AA920 was transferred to No 124 Squadron at RAF Biggin Hill in Kent and continued with this unit until 31st August 1942, when it was transferred to No 71 (Eagle) Squadron at RAF Debden in Essex.

On 29th September 1942, No 71 Squadron was disbanded and re-designated as 334th Squadron, 4th Pursuit Group, USAAF; RAF Debden now became Station 356. The squadron's aircraft were used to escort B-17 Flying Fortress and B-24 Liberator bombers on daylight raids over northern Germany and AA920 would have almost certainly been one of the aircraft involved. However, after another accident it was returned to Air Service Training Ltd at RAF Hamble in Hampshire on 24th November 1942 for repair, overhaul and modification.

Passed fit for service once again on 1st February 1943, the Spitfire was delivered by air to No 15 Maintenance Unit on 14th February and then on to No 222 Squadron at Martlesham Heath in Suffolk. On 31st May it arrived at RAF Westhampnett in Sussex for No 167 Squadron, which just twelve days later was renumbered as No 322 (Dutch) Squadron.

After some nine months of relative stability with one unit, AA920 was returned to Vickers Armstrong in March 1944. There followed a couple of short stays with No 1 Squadron before the Spitfire joined No 402 (Winnipeg Bear) Squadron, Royal Canadian Air Force on 5th June 1944 in order to provide cover for the D-Day landings. This was to be perhaps AA920's finest hour because the next assignment, to No 57 OTU at RAF Eshott in Northumberland on 20th July 1944, would prove to be its last.

The Crash

At 09.05 hours on 18th April 1945, Flight Sergeant Edwin Pannett took off from RAF Eshott in Spitfire VB AA920 having been tasked to carry out a height climb to 2,500 feet and then practise aerobatics during the descent. His flying career had begun with flying training at No 18 Elementary Flying Training School (EFTS) at Fairoaks in Kent on 26th January 1942, following which he was posted to Nos 32, 34 and 35 EFTS in Canada where he flew Harvards and was assessed as an average pilot.

After his return to England, Flight Sergeant Pannett completed his flying training with No 28 EFTS on 10th May 1943 and was posted to No 5 Advanced Flying Unit on 14th May, where he flew the Miles Master and was assessed as average but over-confident in formation flying. He then served with No 290 Squadron, accumulating 220 flying hours on Miles Martinets (possibly on target-towing duties) before being posted to No 595 Squadron from 1st October 1944 to 24th March 1945. He then joined No 57 OTU at RAF Eshott in April 1945. He was assessed as a proficient pilot of single-engined aircraft, with a total of 740 hours 45 minutes which included 11 hours on the Spitfire.

Eyewitnesses stated that the Spitfire had good height when Flight Sergeant Pannett began his aerobatic manoeuvres. The aircraft entered a slow roll to the right and then began to dive, the air speed increasing rapidly until, at approximately 300–400 feet, Pannett attempted to pull out of the dive. At this point, at 09.15 hours, just ten minutes after take-off, the Spitfire was seen to start to disintegrate.

Mr. Jas C. Parker of the Northumberland Special Constabulary appears to have been the closest eyewitness. He stated that his attention was drawn to the plane because it seemed to be in difficulty, with the engine missing badly. He saw three or four black objects fall from the aircraft, immediately after which there was an explosion and several parts of the aircraft came down in two fields.

Lance Corporal G. H. Clark of the Sherwood Foresters saw the Spitfire go 'into a shallow dive', straighten out, turn on its back and then roll back to the normal flying position. 'It then went directly into a steep dive and the engine began to roar,' said Clark. After it had dived for some distance he saw a 'large piece fly up from the right-hand side', followed by pieces which appeared to fly out from the engine. Lance Corporal Clark stated that he did not hear an explosion; but he was maybe two miles from the crash, and it could be argued that the sound did not carry that far.

A third eyewitness witness basically confirmed what Mr Parker and Lance Corporal Clark had said.

The Aftermath

Wing Commander W. D. Coleman from No 57 OTU investigated the crash site on the day of the accident and found that the cockpit, a small part of the fuselage and part of the port wing were the only parts located in one spot. The engine, which had buried itself six feet into the ground, was at least twenty feet away and half the starboard wing was some 400 yards away, back along the line of flight. As he walked further back, Wing Commander Coleman found parts of the starboard wing, and finally the rear of the fuselage. The wreckage was spread over an area 200 yards wide and three-quarters of a mile long.

The cause of the crash was clear to see: severe stress had been placed on the root of the wing, so that when Flight Sergeant Pannett carried out his manoeuvre the wing separated from the root and folded back, wrecking the fuselage and the tail. The Spitfire had been judged airworthy before the flight, but Pannett was not in the air long enough to carry out any aggressive manoeuvres.

It is my belief that the stress AA920's airframe had endured during its long flying career (at the time of the crash it had flown for 923 hours 35 minutes) has to be seriously considered as a causal factor in the weakening of the airframe, the result of which was this fatal accident just north-west of Longhorsley in Northumberland.

The Crash Site

The last resting place of Spitfire AA920 – or at least the engine – is still evident and is defined by a crater some ten to fifteen feet in diameter. The area of the crash is not very far outside Longhorsley and you can drive virtually all the way to the site itself. The last few yards, however, is through a field full of sheep and is private land on which permission to enter must be granted by the landowner.

Russell Gray

The crash site, looking back from where the engine was found. (R.Gray)

More remains of Spitfire AA920 removed from the crash site some years ago. (R.Gray)

27

Supermarine Spitfire IXF MH388

Aircraft Type:	**Supermarine Spitfire IX**
Serial:	MH388
Code(s):	CM
Unit:	No 80 Operational Training Unit
Base:	RAF Ouston, Northumberland
Crew:	Pilot: Commandant Christian Martell (Lucien Montet)
Crash Date:	31st August 1945
Crash Location:	RAF Ouston, Northumberland
Grid Reference:	88/073701

The Aircraft

The Spitfire IX was actually a beefed-up Mk V with a 1,560 hp Merlin 61, which entered service as a stop-gap measure to counter the formidable FW 190. Although the differences in performance between the Mk V and Mk IX were considerable, their similarities in appearance meant that German pilots had difficulty in spotting the difference until it was too late. Among the all-important distinguishing features that identified the Spitfire IX were a four-bladed Rotol propeller, a slightly longer nose, symmetrical glycol, oil and intercooler radiators beneath the wings, metal-skinned ailerons and a broader rudder.

The new engine could hold power up to far greater altitudes; in fact it had twice the power at 30,000 feet of the early Merlins. Maximum speed was 408 mph. Armament consisted of four .303 calibre machine guns and two 20mm cannons, or two .50 calibre machine guns and two 20mm cannons in the Mk IXE. Two 500-pound bombs and rocket projectiles could also be carried.

A computer-generated picture of Spitfire MH388 (Simon Glancy)

Given the fact that the Spitfire IX was a stop-gap fighter, the production total of 5,656 aircraft (plus 282 Mk V conversions) is quite remarkable. It entered service with No 64 Squadron at RAF Hornchurch in Essex in July 1942 and still equipped eight squadrons on home defence duties in May 1945. Another five squadrons within 2nd Tactical Air Force in Europe were similarly equipped, as were 22 squadrons of the Desert and Balkan Air Forces. The last examples were retired from RAF service in 1947.

The Crash

On 31st August 1945 Commandant Christian Martell took off from RAF Ouston in Northumberland in Spitfire IXF MH388. He and his aircraft were assigned to No 80 Operational Training Unit which was tasked with training French pilots for the four Spitfire squadrons of 2nd Tactical Air Force. The unit was initially based at RAF Morpeth but had moved to RAF Ouston the previous month.

The pilot of Spitfire MH338, Christian Martell. (Roger Borne)

Christian Martell's real name was Lucien Montet. He was born in St Etienne in France on 14th March 1914 and by the age of 23 was a sergeant pilot in the 'Etampes' aerobatic squadron of the French Air Force. By the time war broke out, he was supervisor at Romily Air Combat School, but desperate to join a combat squadron. Instead he was kept where he was, promotion to sub-lieutenant in April 1940 being of little consolation.

After the fall of France, Montet was demobilised but remained eager to continue the fight under General de Gaulle, so he set sail aboard the SS *Le Saint Pierre*, heading for Gibraltar and the RAF. Unfortunately the ship was captured by the Spanish Army after being washed ashore off Ibiza and Montet was arrested and imprisoned by the Vichy police. He was eventually provisionally set free and escaped, and on 9th April 1942 he arrived in London. It was then that he decided to take the *nom de guerre* of Christian Martell, after the cognac, for fear of reprisals against his family in France.

On the understanding that he would be placed with an RAF squadron, he agreed to first be parachuted back into France to set up an escape network which he then handed over to his brother Maurice. He returned to England in late 1942 and trained once more as a combat pilot, then joined No 341 (Alsace) Squadron of the Free French Air Forces in January 1943.

The squadron had been formed at RAF Turnhouse in Scotland on 15th January 1941 by Free French personnel and was equipped with Spitfire VBs; but by March it had started to receive Spitfire IXs and Martell quickly mastered the new aircraft. On 27th July 1943 he destroyed two FW 190s; another double kill (a Bf 109 and a FW 190) followed on 22nd September. By December 1943 Martell had taken command of the squadron which began to concentrate on ground attack, destroying enemy transport in a prelude to the invasion of mainland France: Operation 'Overlord'. At war's end he had flown 151 offensive missions and was an ace with six 'kills' and six probables.

My account of the crash of MH388 is based entirely on the eyewitness accounts of Glyn and Dick Robinson. Glyn was no more than twenty yards from the scene at the time of the accident and recalled that he and a friend were walking across the field towards his sister who was picking blackberries. Dick was in the house having tea, which puts the time at approximately 16.30 hours, when they noticed a Spitfire approaching from the north-west, its engine seriously misfiring.

The pilot was heading for RAF Ouston and Glyn was sure the Spitfire was going to miss the trees, but it was not to be. The aircraft clipped the first

The burning remains of Spitfire MH388 after the crash. **(Icare)**

tree and then flew straight into the second, which ripped off the wing and caused an explosion of wood and branches. 'I saw branches flying into the sky and an aeroplane minus its wing coming through the tree,' recalled Glyn. 'It skidded about 100 yards and immediately caught fire ... the plane was inverted.' As soon as the Spitfire came to rest the flames shot back along the track of the aircraft, which seems to confirm suggestions that the fuel tank had been ruptured; it was propelled up and into the tree, immediately extinguishing itself.

Unfortunately the same did not happen with the Spitfire which was lying inverted, on fire and with Christian Martell trapped inside the cockpit. It took only a few minutes for the French ground crew from 'B' Flight to get to the scene, but they were precious seconds because the flames were by then very fierce. The ground crew gallantly tried to extract Martell from the cockpit, many of them being badly burned in the process, and eventually the aircraft was raised just enough to pull him free.

The Aftermath

Christian Martell was whisked away in an ambulance, but he died twenty minutes later on his way to the hospital. Glyn and Dick remember that either the next day or the day after that a Dakota landed at RAF Ouston and Martell's body was taken aboard and returned to France, where he was buried in the Père Lachaise Cemetery in Paris.

The Crash Site

Nothing now remains of MH388 at the crash site, there being no hint that an accident even took place; the area, as with that where Hampden I L4054 crashed (see Chapter 11), has been continuously farmed since the war. In addition, the Spitfire struck a tree and crashed from a low altitude, so no deep remains could be expected; it did not explode and there were plenty of personnel from nearby RAF Ouston to help with the clear-up. But there have been finds over the years, notably the tail wheel and an exploded cannon shell, both of which were recovered by Glyn and Dick. My colleague Mike Farrer and I searched the area in 2006 and found small fragments which by their nature could only have come from an aircraft crash site. We are hoping to display these and any other finds as a tribute to Free French pilot, Christian Martell.

Russell Gray

The Spitfire 'skidded about 100 yards and immediately caught fire ...' **(Icare)**

28

Vickers Varsity T1 WL640

Aircraft Type:	**Vickers Varsity T1**
Serial:	WL640
Code(s):	W
Unit:	No 2 Air Navigation School, RAF
Base:	RAF Thorney Island, Hampshire
Crew:	Pilot: Flight Sergeant Thomas Garlick Navigator: Flight Lieutenant Frederick R. Lambeth Signaller: Sergeant Alan R. J. Turner Student Navigator: Flight Lieutenant John Page Student Navigator: Pilot Officer Robert G. Gaymer
Crash Date:	20th September 1957
Crash Location:	White Hill, Falstone, Northumberland
Grid Reference:	80/756873

The Aircraft

In the years following the Second World War, the RAF started to develop new aircraft to replace types that had served very well throughout the war years but which needed to be replaced. One such type was the Wellington bomber (see Chapter 29) which, following its withdrawal from front-line duties, went on to serve as RAF Bomber Command's principal crew trainer. This role continued post-war, when Wellington T10s (converted Mk Xs) were assigned to Air Navigation Schools (ANS) and No 201 Advanced Flying School (AFS) within RAF Flying Training Command. It was clear, however, that future RAF aircrew selected for multi-engine training would require a more up-to-date crew trainer and this requirement formed the basis of Air Ministry Specification C9/46.

During the mid-1940s, Vickers developed the Viking (the origins of which lay in the Wellington) for commercial use as a medium/short-haul airliner. Four examples were acquired by the RAF for use as Viking CIIs in the King's (later Queen's) Flight from 1947; but the RAF, aware of the Viking's success as an airliner, saw its potential as a military transport. With this in mind larger engines were fitted, the floor was strengthened, and large loading doors were added in the port side of the fuselage to produce the Vickers Valetta.

The Valetta C1 transport entered RAF service in 1948 and proved to be very versatile. Subsequent development included the T3 navigator trainer, 40 of which replaced Wellington T10s in the Air Navigation Schools during 1950/1. However the need for a new crew trainer, outlined in Air Ministry Specification T13/48, remained. The answer lay in further development of the Valetta. The aircraft was remodelled with a tricycle undercarriage, the nose was lengthened, and the wing-span was increased by six feet. In addition, a long pannier beneath the fuselage contained a work position for trainee bomb aimers (forward section) and up to 24 small practice bombs (rear section).

The new crew trainer, appropriately named the Varsity, flew on 17th July 1949 when the prototype (VX828) made its first flight. The first production Varsity T1 flew on 21st May 1951 and entered RAF service on 1st October the same year when it was accepted by No 201 AFS at RAF Swinderby in Lincolnshire. The Varsity was the perfect training aircraft for the RAF; able to accommodate pilots, navigators, flight engineers, radio operators and bomb aimers for training purposes.

When production ceased in February 1954, 163 Varsity T1s had been built. As well as replacing the Wellington T10s in No 201 AFS, they replaced Valetta T3s in No 1 ANS at RAF Stradishall in Suffolk and No 2 ANS at RAF Gaydon in Warwickshire (later, RAF Thorney Island in Hampshire). The Varsity T1 remained in service until May 1976 when the last examples with No 5 Flying Training School at RAF Oakington in Cambridgeshire were replaced by Handley Page Jetstream T1s.

The Crash

The hills and moors around Kielder Reservoir in Northumberland are quiet, peaceful areas used for leisure activities, pastoral farming and a range of forestry activities. To the south-east of the reservoir, above the small village of Falstone, moors give way to large plantations of conifers; recent additions to the landscape. It was on these peaceful moors, just over 50 years ago, that five young airmen lost their lives.

At 17.45 hours on 20th September 1957, Varsity T1 WL640 of No 2 ANS at RAF Thorney Island took off for what would be its final flight. On board was a crew of five: pilot, Flight Sergeant Thomas Garlick, aged 37, from Durham; navigator, Flight Lieutenant Frederick Lambeth, also 37 and from Welling in Kent; and signaller, Sergeant Alan Turner, 20, from Cosham in Hampshire. The two remaining crewmen – Flight Lieutenant John Page, 26, of Northfleet in Kent; and Pilot Officer Robert Gaymer, 20, of Theydon Bois in Essex – were both navigators and are assumed to have been on board to complete for training purposes.

Forty-five minutes before WL640 took off, the five crewmen were briefed to carry out navigational training involving a night cross-country flight over Great Britain. The planned route took them from their base at Thorney Island to Llanelli, Carlisle, Morpeth, and then back to Thorney Island, with orders to fly at 13,000 feet to avoid commercial airways. Their aircraft had first joined No 2 ANS at Thorney Island on 12th December 1956; prior to that it had been issued to No 8 Maintenance Unit on 18th June 1953 from its makers, Vickers Armstrong Ltd of Weybridge in Surrey. While at No 2 ANS it had been occupied with training flights, and had managed to accumulate 258 flying hours by the time of its first minor inspection in June 1957. The flying time had increased to 459 hours 35 minutes (and 302 landings) by the time WL640 departed at the start of what was a routine training exercise that ended in tragedy.

Exactly what happened remains uncertain to this day; however, it would appear that the aircraft successfully completed the first leg (Thorney Island to Llanelli) and the second leg (Llanelli to Carlisle) of the exercise. After reaching Carlisle it changed direction to head for Morpeth, and it was while on this third leg of the flight that things went horrifically wrong. At 19.45 hours, two hours after take-off, Varsity T1 WL640 hit Thorneyburn Common above Falstone spreading wreckage over some 1½ miles.

Crashed 20th September 1957

Thorney Burn, where the largest parts of Varsity WL640 ended up.
(Public Record Office)

The starboard side of the cockpit section of Varsity WL640 taken after the crash. While this half remained quite complete, the port side was very badly damaged. (Public Record Office)

On the evening of the accident, farm worker John Weir was at home when he became aware of an aircraft coming down over his house at Hawkehope; then he heard the impact as it crashed and spread itself over the moor behind his house. A newspaper reported at the time how it was John Weir's directions that led the rescue services to within 50 yards of the main site of wreckage. Over the following two days RAF personnel, police, fire crews and forestry workers searched the fell side in atrocious weather in an attempt to locate all of the wreckage.

The Varsity's cockpit and the main central section of the fuselage had come to rest about 60 yards apart in the Thorney Burn on the western side of Thorney Burn Fell. Slightly downhill and to the south-east, the two Bristol Hercules engines were located, partly embedded in the moor; the remaining wreckage lay broken up and scattered over the higher ground to the north-west of Thorney Burn, spreading up to the forest plantation. In all, the main wreckage was spread over 1½ miles of moorside, with lighter objects such as soundproofing material and maps even further afield in the woodland two miles from the cockpit.

All five of the crew had died instantly. Flight Lieutenant Lambeth and Sergeant Turner were discovered in the wreckage of the cockpit; Flight Lieutenant Page was found in between the cockpit and the fuselage; the pilot, Flight Sergeant Garlick, was found approximately 40 yards south-east of the cockpit, near the stream; and Pilot Officer Gaymer lay some 80 yards to the west of the cockpit, on the moorside, having been thrown the furthest.

The Aftermath

In the weeks that followed a detailed investigation took place into the circumstances of the crash. The RAF sent a team to examine and photograph the wreckage where it lay; members of the group, headed by the senior investigator Mr A. E. R. Broomfield, stayed at the Black Cock Inn at Falstone. Their work included carrying out a wreckage plot to determine in which direction the aircraft had been flying. By 27th September most of the on-site work had been completed, and the task of transporting the remains of WL640 to the Royal Aircraft Establishment at Farnborough in Hampshire had begun. Once there, the wreckage was reconstructed and thoroughly examined.

By early 1958 an initial report had been filed with findings from the investigation; but it was not until later that year that the full report was completed. The findings stated that the aircraft had suffered structural failure in flight, with both port and starboard wings failing under download. Both wings had broken off just outboard of the engines, after which both engines became detached. Nose and tail downloads had led to stressing along the upper fuselage, which caused the fuselage structure to fail, initially over the wing centre section. However it was the rear section of the fuselage that broke up; the main forward section remained largely intact. It is believed that the breaking up of the rear section was secondary to the loss of all the elevators (flaps), which had been rotated to hard up, possibly in an attempt by the pilot to regain control.

A study of the wreckage trail suggested that the Varsity had been flying on a course of 170 degrees, and had suffered structural failure at an altitude of 5–8,000 feet. As it was known that the aircraft was supposed to be flying at 13,000 feet, it could been assumed that loss of control had occurred causing the aircraft to lose at least 5,000 feet of height, and that the resulting stress on the airframe had resulted in the structural failure. But what had caused the loss of control?

It was noted that, when the bodies of the five crewmen were recovered from the crash site, the pilot's seat was not occupied by Flight Sergeant

***The site of the crash today, where small fragments still lie amongst the reeds and heather.* (J. Shipley)**

Garlick, but by the signaller, Sergeant Turner. What happened while Turner was in the pilot's seat will never be known, but tests on the aircraft's autopilot suggested that it was fully functioning and was not to blame.

Why Garlick had left his seat remains a mystery. He was an extremely experienced pilot, so it can be assumed that he felt able to do so without putting the aircraft and its occupants in any danger. At the age of 37, he had amassed some 3,638 flying hours on various types (including 1,268 on the Varsity), was an instructor category A2, and at his last assessment had been rated 'above average'. His expertise as a pilot was also voiced by his Commanding Officer, who stated in the final report: 'He was a competent and reliable pilot and a captain of high calibre, and it was not in his character to disregard instructions without justification.' The CO went on to suggest that, 'when he left his seat he was taking a legitimate calculated risk of captaincy, possibly to inspect something unusual in the back of the aircraft'.

What actually caused the Varsity to break up will never be known. What is certain is that, in the hours that followed the crash, wives, parents and relatives of the five dead airmen received the news they had always dreaded. Flight Sergeant Garlick, Flight Lieutenant Lambeth, Sergeant Turner and Pilot Officer Gaymer were laid to rest together in Saint Nicholas's churchyard, near RAF Thorney Island, while Flight Lieutenant Page was buried in Saint Peter's churchyard in the village of Merton in Norfolk.

The Crash Site

As a result of Varsity WL640 breaking up in mid-air and scattering wreckage over a large area, one cannot really provide a single location for the crash site today. The grid reference mentioned is centered on the cockpit area which came to rest in Thorney Burn; however nothing large now remains at that location.

The peacetime recovery operation was extremely thorough, and almost all wreckage was collected for the investigation that followed. Added to this, large areas of the moor, which had been covered with the wreckage of WL640, have now been planted with trees creating a near-impregnable forest. However, small parts of the Varsity can still be located across the moor, while small fragments appear when the trees are felled, and the hillside is ploughed in advance of new trees being planted.

Jonathan Shipley

29

Vickers Wellington IC X3171

Aircraft Type:	**Vickers Wellington IC**
Serial:	X3171
Code(s):	NOT KNOWN
Unit:	No 15 Operational Training Unit
Base:	RAF Harwell, Oxfordshire
Crew:	Pilot: Sergeant David L. Barley Bomb aimer: Pilot Officer Joseph Donnelly Bomb aimer: Pilot Officer Thomas Winstanley Wireless Operator/Air Gunner: Dennis R. Bending Navigator: Sergeant William S. Gibson Air Gunner: Sergeant George Marshall
Crash Date:	1st March 1943
Crash Location:	Comb Moor, Northumberland
Grid Reference:	80/772930

The Aircraft

The Wellington was the result of Vickers' response to Air Ministry Specification B9/32, which called for a high-performance twin-engined medium bomber able to carry a good bomb load at speed. The new aircraft were to be monoplanes and would replace biplane bombers then in service. Designs from Handley Page and Vickers were accepted and constructed in prototype form.

The Vickers design first flew in prototype form (K4049) on 15th June 1936, six days before the Handley Page prototype. Exactly two months later the Air Ministry placed initial orders for 180 production Wellington Is and a similar number of the Handley Page design, which became the

Hampden I (see Chapter 11). The first Wellington I (L4212) flew on 23rd December 1937, some six months before the first Hampden I, and together these two bombers, along with the Armstrong Whitworth Whitley (see Chapter 1), formed the backbone of RAF Bomber Command in the early years of the Second World War.

A Wellington from the collection of Vaclav Kolesa.
(via Pavel Vancata)

The most interesting aspect of the Wellington's design was its geodetic construction. This was the brainchild of Barnes Wallis and comprised a diagonal lattice-work of alloy members which provided considerable structural strength. This enabled the Wellington to soak up an immense amount of damage without compromising the structural integrity of the aircraft, and thus allowed many damaged Wellingtons and their six-man crews to make it safely back home. (As for we aviation archaeologists, the distinctive lattice-work can be the first indication that we have found a Wellington as opposed to any other type of aircraft.)

The Wellington Mk I differed from the prototype in a number of ways, the most notable being a redesigned fuselage to allow for Vickers nose and tail gun turrets and a Nash & Thompson retractable ventral 'dustbin' turret, each armed with twin .303 calibre machine guns. The fabric-covered geodetic structure also saved weight, which allowed the bomber to carry a heavier bomb load for a greater distance: 4,500 pounds for 1,200 miles. The two Pegasus XVIII radial engines gave the Wellington a maximum speed of 235 mph.

The first of 183 Wellington Is to be built entered service with No 99 Squadron at RAF Mildenhall in Suffolk in October 1938. By the outbreak of war on 3rd September 1939, all 183 had been delivered to equip eight Bomber Command squadrons. The next day, fourteen Wellington Is from Nos 9 and 149 Squadrons, in conjunction with Blenheims, became the first RAF bombers to attack Germany with an attack on warships at Brunsbüttel.

Crashed 1st March 1943

Later daylight raids included the participation of Wellington IAs (187 built), which had the two Vickers manually-operated turrets replaced by Nash & Thompson power-operated turrets. However, the Wellington's weakness was attack from abeam, and attempts to address this problem led to the Wellington IC in which the ventral turret was replaced by two single .303 calibre machine guns that could be fired from the rear of the fuselage glazing. The Mk IC, 2,685 of which were built (almost 25 per cent of total Wellington production), entered service in April 1940 and by the end of the year equipped no less than nineteen squadrons in Bomber Command.

During 1941 the Mk IC began to give way to Wellington IIs and IIIs and the first of Bomber Command's four-engined 'heavies'. Many of the survivors were assigned to training units, but they were called back into action for the first and second of Air Marshall Harris's three '1,000' bomber raids in mid-1942.

Vickers Wellington IC X3171 was manufactured by Vickers Armstrong Ltd at their Squire's Gate factory near Blackpool and, although it never served with an operational squadron, it did see front-line service in two of the most destructive raids of the Second World War.

The aircraft was first issued to No 23 Maintenance Unit at RAF Aldergrove near Belfast on 3rd March 1941, after which it was transferred on 20th April to the Royal Aircraft Establishment (RAE) at Farnborough in Hampshire. There it was fitted with a cine-camera for reconnaissance work with No 3 Photographic Reconnaissance Unit. This equipment was removed on 30th June and X3171 was transferred to the Aeroplane & Armament Experimental Establishment at Boscombe Down in Wiltshire, on detachment from the RAE, for night photography trials. After completion of the trials work, X3171 was passed on to No 10 Maintenance Unit at RAF Hullavington in Wiltshire on 26th October 1941; then on again, this time to No 15 Operational Training Unit at RAF Harwell in Oxfordshire on 6th March 1942.

After a minor accident on 11th May this well-travelled 'Wimpey' was drafted into front-line service on the night of 30th/31st May 1942, when it was flown by Flight Sergeant A. R. Middleton as one of twenty Wellingtons from RAF Harwell that participated in the first '1,000' bomber raid, also known as the 'thousand plan', on Cologne in Germany. (No less than 599 of the bombers that took part that night were Wellingtons.) The squadron also participated in the second '1,000' bomber raid, this time on the night of 1st/2nd June 1942, when 28 Wellingtons, one of which was X3171, again piloted by Middleton, struck Essen.

Wellington IC X3171 came through both of these massive raids quite unscathed, and apart from routine training flights nothing really happened to the aircraft until 1st March 1943; except that is for a peculiar incident on 10th August 1942 when, during a routine training/navigational flight between Filey and St Abbs Head on the eastern coast of England, the tail gunner, Canadian Sergeant Robert Duff Bijur, mysteriously bailed out of the aircraft. To this day no one knows why he did so. His body was never recovered and so he is remembered today on Panel 107 of the Runnymede Memorial in Surrey, which commemorates all those who lost their lives during the Second World War whilst serving with the Air Forces of the Commonwealth at bases in Great Britain or in north-western Europe, and who have no known grave.

The Crash

At around 11.00 hours on 1st March 1943, Wellington IC X3171 took off from RAF Harwell for a solo cross-country flight. Nothing is really known about the flight, but at 15.00 hours the aircraft crashed into a peat bog nine miles north-west of Bellingham in Northumberland. All six members of the crew were killed.

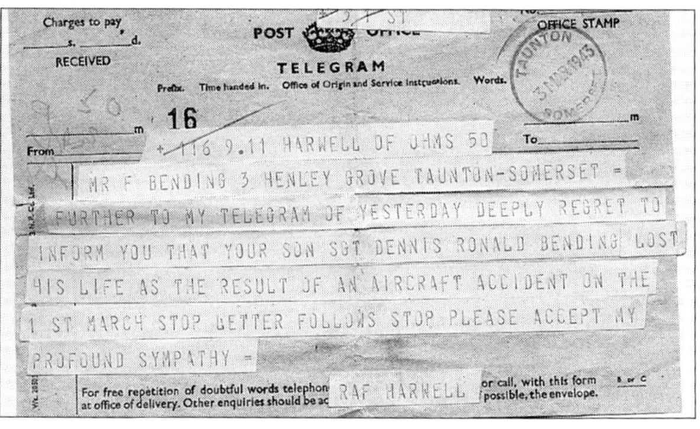

Charges to pay s. d.
RECEIVED
POST OFFICE
TELEGRAM
OFFICE STAMP
Prefix. Time handed in. Office of Origin and Service Instructions. Words.
16
From + 116 9.11 HARWELL OF OHMS 50 To
MR F BENDING 3 HENLEY GROVE TAUNTON-SOMERSET =
FURTHER TO MY TELEGRAM OF YESTERDAY DEEPLY REGRET TO
INFORM YOU THAT YOUR SON SGT DENNIS RONALD BENDING LOST
HIS LIFE AS THE RESULT OF AN AIRCRAFT ACCIDENT ON THE
1 ST MARCH STOP LETTER FOLLOWS STOP PLEASE ACCEPT MY
PROFOUND SYMPATHY =
RAF HARWELL
For free repetition of doubtful words telephon... at office of delivery. Other enquiries should be ac... or call, with this form ... possible, the envelope.

The telegram relaying the sad news about Dennis Bending. **(The Bending family)**

The aircraft was reportedly seen on fire prior to the crash by a shepherd at Emblehope who reported the incident to the Royal Observer Corps post at 18.30 hours. Why did so much time pass between the time of the crash and the shepherd's reporting of it? There are two possibilities: either because he first walked to the scene of the crash before reporting it, or because the lack of telephones in the immediate area meant that he had to walk some distance before he was able to raise the alarm.

The Crash Site

This site remained undiscovered for some 62 years, until some wreckage was found by ACIA's Jim Corbett and Chris Johnson of the North East Aircraft Museum. This consisted of an oxygen bottle and numerous small fragments, but that was all. Any other small parts were assumed to have been thrown clear by the explosion that occurred after X3171 crashed.

On 2nd February 2005 an area 100 yards in radius from the point where the oxygen bottle had been found was scoured and yielded some new finds. At a point some 100 yards south-west of the oxygen bottle were four shallow water-filled pits, and a more detailed search of these produced a large concentration of finds heading down the slope. These pits were surveyed in more detail on 16th April 2005 by Nick Wotherspoon of the Lancashire Aviation Investigation Team; work which proved that the pits were made by the Wellington and that there were substantial remains still buried beneath the surface. Based on this evidence an application was made to the Ministry of Defence for a licence to allow us to recover X3171, and this was granted on 29th June 2005.

The excavation work was carried out in two stages: a hand dig to find and locate the smaller items of interest and to try to establish where the larger parts were located; then a machine dig with an excavator to remove and recover all larger parts such as engines, propellers etc. By locating and plotting the smaller pieces of identifiable wreckage, we could get a better idea of wreckage distribution and therefore an orientation of the aircraft when it crashed.

On 8th August 2005, armed with spades and midge nets, we began to dig test trenches. Small fragments of the aircraft were immediately discovered and as we reached greater depths the parts increased in size and quantity. However, as the day wore on it became obvious that a mechanical excavator was needed if we were to have a realistic chance of continuing the recovery. This was duly acquired and a full-scale machine dig began, ably assisted by the known relatives of the aircrew (who had been invited to the crash site) and a host of helpers to sort out the spoil as it was removed.

Atrocious weather hampered the excavation of the site where the Wellington came down.

The morning of the dig was bright and sunny and everyone was filled with anticipation. The excavator arrived early and was nearly in position when the rest of us arrived. Once all the necessary safety measures were in place, the machine dig commenced and very soon we began to recover parts of X3171. The dig continued throughout the day, with the excavator operator constantly being asked to stop when something of interest was detected.

The finds were many and varied: camera spools, fragments of geodetic fuselage, the airspeed indicator; then finally, at a depth of about 15 feet, what we had all been waiting for: a propeller blade and boss. Our exhilaration soon turned to disappointment, however, when it began to dawn on us that this would be one of the last finds. The RAF maintenance unit tasked with cleaning up the site had done its job well; a fact corroborated by a witness statement, received just prior to the dig, which said that an RAF Queen Mary trailer was seen loaded up with wreckage soon after the accident, and that most of it seemed to have been removed from the site.

Happy with what we had found but disappointed that we had not found more, the hole was filled in, fenced off and made safe as part of our contractual agreement with the Forestry Commission. A consolation was the fact that one of the families in attendance, the Bendings, could finally be told that their uncle Dennis, one of the six crewmen who perished in the crash, had indeed been correctly buried and was not still with the aircraft.

A memorial plaque to the six crewmen was unveiled on 4th November 2006 at the Hollybush Inn at Greenhaugh by Len Lambert, a childhood friend of the navigator, Sergeant William Gibson, and Aidan Donnelly, the great-great-nephew of the bomb aimer, Pilot Officer Joseph Donnelly.

In conclusion, we are still not entirely convinced that we have found all of the wreckage, especially as there are rumours that local children have played on a set of aircraft wings on the other side of the hill. Obviously this still has to be verified – such rumours prevail in local legend around many air crashes. A display of items that have been found so far can be viewed at the North East Aircraft Museum in Sunderland.

Russell Gray

The main find of the day – the propeller blade and boss. **(R. Gray)**

CREDITS & REFERENCE SOURCES

Armstrong Whitworth Whitley V P4952
Mark Niman
Peter Clark
Jim Rutland
Brian Anderson
Paul Cummings
Air Ministry Form 1180 (Accident Card)
Air Ministry Form 78 (Movement Card)

Avro Vulcan B2 XM610
Jim Rutland
Thetford, O. (1988) *Aircraft of the Royal Air Force since 1918*, Putnam: London
North East Aircraft Museum

Blackburn Botha Is W5137 and W5154
Mr S. Muller
Air Ministry Form 78 (Movement Card) Botha W5137
Air Ministry Form 78 (Movement Card) Botha W5154
Air Ministry Form 1180 (Loss Card) Botha W5137 and W5154 Collision
PRO – AVIA29/590 4 Air Gunnery School Operational Records Book
Wixey, K. (1997) *Forgotten Bombers of the RAF*, Arms and Armour Press: London

Boeing B-17F-80BO Flying Fortress 42-30030
Ross McNeil
Tisha Carpenter
Victor Torti
Michael Antalek
Derek Walton
Mike Stowe
388 Bomb Group Assoc.

Boeing B-17G-55DL Flying Fortress 44-6504
Carol Kyle Sage
George Anderson Kyle
Joel Berly
Jay & Jeri Hardy
College Valley Estates
Craig Fuller
Mike Stowe
US Air Force
303rd Bomb Group Association
Tim Kent
Simon Glancey
Tina Elliott
Geoff Holland
Family of Bertrand Hallum
USAF Accident Reports
RAF Ouston Station Log
RAF Acklington Station Log
Hexham Courant
Newcastle Chronicle & Journal
Hunters, Martin W. Bowman
The Met Office

Bristol Beaufighter IIF T3037
Mrs Defty
PRO – AVIA27/1791 406 Squadron Operational Records Book
Air Ministry Form 78 (Movement Card) Beaufighter T3037
The *Daily Gleaner*, Saturday 7th September 1940
Air Ministry Form 1180 (Loss Card) Beaufighter T3037
Bingham, V. (1994) *Bristol Beaufighter*, Airlife: Shrewsbury
Chorlton, M. (2005) *Airfields of the North-East of England in the Second World War*, Countryside Books: Newbury
Clark, P. (2002) *Their Corner of a Foreign Field*, Glen Graphics: Wooler
Lloyd's War Losses, the Second World War: Volume 1, Lloyd's of London Press; London

Bristol Beaufort I L9797
Mr R. McNeill
Mr J. Slaughter
Mrs I. Stephen
Air Ministry Form 78 (Movement Card)

Beaufort L9797
Air Ministry Form 1180 (Loss Card) Beaufort L9797
PRO – AVIA27/278 22 Squadron Operational Records Book
Wixey, K. (1997) *Forgotten Bombers of the RAF*, Arms and Armour Press: London

De Havilland DH89A Dragon Rapide G-AFMF
Richard Waugh
Margaret Davidson
Pauline Nicholson
Air Accident Investigation Branch
Official Accident Report
Hexham Courant
Newcastle Chronicle & Journal
Air Ministry Form 78 (Movement Card)

De Havilland Venom FB4 WR557
Accident Investigation Branch Memo. S. 2869
Air Ministry Form 1180 (Loss Card) Venom WR557
RAF Commands website.
The Cumberland News
Thetford, O. (1988) *Aircraft of the Royal Air Force since 1918*, Putnam: London

Fairey Flycatcher Is N9677 & N9679
Margaret Massham
Ivan Wright
Derek Walton
Peter Clark
Ray Sturtivant
Malcolm Fillmore
Willie Grimwood
Alastair Murray
Hexham Courant

Handley Page Hampden I L4054
The family of Denis Sharpe
National Archives AVIA5/19 folio W749
New Zealand Defence Force, Personnel Archives
RAF Commands Forum
Chorley, W. R. (1996) *Bomber Command Losses Volume 2, 1940*
Moyes, P. J. R. (1965) *The Handley Page Hampden*, Profile Publications

Hawker Hunter F6A XG236
Peter Clark
Robert Anderson
Scott McIntosh
Karl Edmondson
Steve Wild
David Armstrong
Tim Heath
Martin W. Bowman
Alastair Aked (former 66sqn pilot)
Terry Kingsley (former 66sqn pilot)
Margaret Schooling Ballast
Reg Schooling
Forest Enterprise Kielder
66 Squadron Operational Record Book
Air Ministry Form 1180 (Accident Card)
Air Ministry Form 78 (Movement Card)
Summary of the Board of Inquiry

Hawker Hurricane IV KX190
John Gates
Chris Davies
Keith Maddison
Mr and Mrs Foti
John Colton
Walter Eacott
Air Ministry Form 1180 (Accident Card)
Air Ministry Form 78 (Movement Card)
John Gates Personnel File

Hawker Tempest V EJ859
Colin Burgess: Author of *Bush Parker – An Australian Battle of Britain Pilot in Colditz*
Alec Thompson: Chester-Le-Street Heritage Group
Cameron and Margaret Martin: Felkington Farm
Judith Jenson: Winolobo Library
Australian Archives
Caroline Anderson: English Literature skills

Hawker Typhoon IB MN140
Mr A. Bar
Mr T. Laidlaw
Air Ministry Form 78 (Movement Card) Typhoon MN140
Air Ministry Form 1180 (Loss Card) Typhoon MN140
PRO – AVIA27/2103 609 Squadron Operational Records Book
PRO – AIR50/171 Combat reports to Charles Detal (five in total)
Bickers, R. T. (1999) *The Hawker Typhoon*, Crowood Press: Marlborough
Earnshaw, J. (2005) *Royal Air Force Pilots Flying Log Book of Squadron Leader "Pinkie" Stark*, privately published by Jim Earnshaw/Artistic Flight

Heinkel He 111H-5 3550
Mr Bill Norman
Mr James Davidson
PRO – AVIA27/141 Squadron Operational Records Book
PRO – AVIA27/132 Squadron Operational Records Book
Norman, B. (2002) *Broken Eagles 2: Luftwaffe Losses over Northumberland and Durham 1939–1945,* Pen & Sword: Barnsley
Ramsey, W. G. (1988) *The Blitz Then and Now: Volume 2,* Battle of Britain Prints: London

Junkers Ju 88A-4 1064
Mr J. Dawson
Mrs Riddell
NRO – NC/6/10 Air Raid Report
PRO – AIR50/139 Combat Report Fumerton
PRO – AIR27/1791 406 Squadron Operational Records Book
Norman, B. (2002) *Broken Eagles 2: Luftwaffe Losses over Northumberland and Durham 1939–1945*, Pen & Sword: Barnsley
Walton, D. (1999) *Northumberland Aviation Diary*, Norav Publications: Seahouses

Lockheed F-104 Starfighter D-8337
Rob Philips
Coen van den Heuvel
Herman van Bruggen
Theo Stoelinga
Malchoir Timmers
Henk Welting
Erwin van Loo

Piper PA28-181 Cherokee Archer II G-BHDG
Peter and Gill Hart
Walter Brown
Sarah Wilson
Peter Clark
Chris Davies
Phil Smith
Official Accident Report
Air Accident Investigation Branch
Newcastle Chronicle & Journal
The Scotsman

Republic P-47D-21RE Thunderbolt 42-25530
PRO–AIR29/683 Proceedings of Court of Inquiry Or Investigation (opened on 14th April 1944)
War Department U. S. Army Air Forces Report of Aircraft Accident (accident number 117)
Green, W. and Swanborough, G. (1994) *The Complete Book of Fighters*, Salamander: London
Jane's Fighting Aircraft of World War II

Short Stirling III EH880
Air Ministry Form 78 (Movement Card) Stirling EH880
PRO – AVIA27/646 75 Squadron Operational Records Book
Bowyer, M. J. F. (2002) *The Short Stirling*, Crecy Publishing Ltd: Manchester
Chorley, W. R. (1996) *Bomber*

Command Losses Volume 4, 1943, Midland Counties Publications: Earl Shilton
Walton, D. (1999) *Northumberland Aviation Diary*, Norav Publications: Seahouses

Supermarine Spitfire IAs R6596 and X4595

Dave Young
Paula Stevens
Colin Burgess
Daniel Spoors
Lawrence Spoors
Gordon Rogerson
Australian Archive: Personnel documents

Supermarine Spitfire IIA P8528

Mr A. Bar
Air Ministry Form 78 (Movement Card) Spifire P8528
Air Ministry Form 1180 (Loss Card) Spitfire P8528
Boot, H. and Sturtivant, R. (2005) *Gifts of War: Presentation Aircraft in Two World Wars*, Air Britain
Haining, P. (1985) *The Spitfire Log*, Souvenir Press: London

Supermarine Spitfire VA P8563

Phil Smith, for his tireless efforts
No 81 Squadron Operational Records Book
RAF Proceedings of Court of Inquiry or Investigation (Flying Accidents) Form 412
Boot, H. and Sturtivant, R. (2005) *Gifts of War: Presentation Aircraft In Two World Wars*, Air Britain
Thetford, O. (1988) *Aircraft of the Royal Air Force since 1918*, Putnam: London

Supermarine Spitfire VB AA920

Mr. W. A. Ricalton
RAF Accident Branch – Report AVIA5/24 – W2178
Freeman, R. *The Mighty Eighth in Colour*
Jefford, Wing Commander C. G. (1988) *RAF Squadrons* Airlife: Shrewsbury
Thetford, O. (1988) *Aircraft of the Royal Air Force since 1918*, Putnam: London

Supermarine Spitfire IXF MH388

Glyn and Dick Robinson
The Order of the Liberation website
Members of The RAF Commands Forum
Green, W. and Swanborough, G. (1994) *The Complete Book of Fighters*, Salamander: London

Vickers Varsity T1 WL640

Air Ministry Form 78 (Movement Card) Varsity WL640
PRO – BT233/394 File regarding loss of Varsity WL640

Vickers Wellington IC X3171

RAF Commands website
Chorley, W. R. (1996) *Bomber Command Losses Volume 4, 1943*, Midland Counties Publications: Earl Shilton
Rapier, B. J. and Bowyer, C. (1995) *Halifax and Wellington*
Thetford, O. (1988) *Aircraft of the Royal Air Force since 1918*, Putnam: London

INDEX